The School of Life:
Stay or Leave

First published in 2021 by The School of Life
First published in the USA in 2022
This paperback edition published in 2024
930 High Road, London, N12 9RT

A proportion of this book has appeared online at
www.theschooloflife.com/articles

Every effort has been made to contact the copyright holders
of the material reproduced in this book. If any have been
inadvertently overlooked, the publisher will be pleased to make
restitution at the earliest opportunity.

The School of Life publishes a range of books on essential topics
in psychological and emotional life, including relationships,
parenting, friendship, careers, and fulfillment. The aim is always
to help us to understand ourselves better—and thereby to grow
calmer, less confused, and more purposeful. Discover our full
range of titles, including books for children, here:
www.theschooloflife.com/books

The School of Life also offers a comprehensive therapy service,
which complements, and draws upon, our published works:
www.theschooloflife.com/therapy

www.theschooloflife.com

ISBN 978-1-915087-51-5

10 9 8 7 6 5 4 3 2 1

The School of Life:
Stay or Leave

How to remain in, or end, your relationship

The School of Life

Contents

Introduction

At points, in despair at yet more agonizing uncertainty about whether it would be best to stay in or to leave a relationship, we might find ourselves harboring a curious longing: that the relationship could be even worse than it is. If, for example, our partner had done something obviously and egregiously appalling, if they were cataclysmically unpleasant and we were unable to stand a single minute more in their presence—in short, if we despised them and they us—it would at least be clear what we should do next.

But our situation is typically complicated by a strange set of facts: that we continue to like our partner at times when we laugh together, that we maintain respect, that they looked very charming the other night, that we think them impressive in company, and that they're superior to ninety-nine percent of the people who cross our path day to day. Maddeningly, try as we might, we can't hate them.

At the same time, we can't rest easy with them either. Whenever we start to relax into the relationship, whenever we finally believe that this could, after all, be the future till the end, something happens to remind us that it can't go on, that this is a fundamentally hopeless situation, that we have to get out while there is still time, that we can't continue to overlook what is wrong between us. It might be the physical relationship or the lack of emotional connection, their refusal to tackle certain inner issues, a maddening argumentativeness, or an absence of warmth or joy. Whatever it may be, the reality is that this is a dysfunctional relationship; we only need to see a properly happy couple to be reminded of all that is humiliatingly amiss.

Stay-or-leave is a lonely place. Society has a lot of patience for people who have been left, and a decent amount of prurient interest in those who are hooking up, but this zone of confusion and ambivalence can feel at once distasteful and tedious. To most of the world, we simply have to put up a brave front and shut up; they largely have no clue how much we ruminate and what pain we're in. We pull a wan smile when they compliment us on our partner and say how happy we look together at the moment (the verdict normally comes just after a particularly grave crisis). It's exhausting to have to pretend to this extent. It may be 3 a.m. before we can look the choice in the eye and feel its full horror staring back.

There may be very few people to whom we can turn. Trusted confidants can be surprisingly thin on the ground; friends may try to hurry us out of the relationship or keep us unnaturally fixed. Behind their advice, we sense their own agendas and experiences muddying the waters.

This book is an attempt to help us out of our inertia. We may be seeking permission to do something we've been longing to do for a while, and hope that a book might provide us with legitimacy. But there may also be cases where the idea of leaving, clearly delineated, provokes disagreement and a fresh appetite for hope and commitment. The best way for us to discover our own taste may be to see what we agree with here and what might provoke spontaneous cries of protest.

After reading this book, we may decide that we do want to stay. Or we may discover that we must have a conversation to end matters in the coming days. Whichever way it goes, what we can hope for above all is resolution. We cannot continue in painful ambivalence indefinitely: We need either to recommit to love (in some form or other) or to abandon it with kindness. At best, either we will stay and now have some firm reasons for doing so, or we will leave, but with a minimum of doubt and a cap on our regrets. This book is a tool that carries the promise of the clearer and less compromised future we deserve.

1
Is it okay to want them to change?

We live in a culture that firmly suggests that the essence of true love is for one person fully to accept the other, as we like to put it, just as they are. In moments of quiet intimacy, the most romantic thing we could ever hear from a partner is, apparently, "I wouldn't change a thing about you," just as the most bitter and disappointed enquiry we could ever throw at a lover in a declining relationship would be: "Why can't you accept me as I am?"

If things do end, we can be guaranteed to garner substantial sympathy from friends and onlookers by explaining that we left because they wanted us to change.

It sounds almost plausible until we pause and modestly remember what the human animal is: a largely demented, broken, agitated, blind, deluded, and barely evolved primate. We are, each one of us, and with nothing derogatory being meant by the term, really rather mad. We are the inheritors of peculiar childhoods; we over- and under-react in a shifting set of areas; we fail to understand key aspects of reality; we get other people wildly wrong; we are unsure of our future; many of our judgments are questionable and a lot of the time we have no idea what is going on.

Against such a background, to insist that there would be nothing about a person that we should want to change, that to be asked to change would be an offense, that we should be loved just as we are feels like the height of arrogance and unreasonableness. Given the facts of human nature, how could we be anything other than profoundly, tirelessly committed to changing a bit here and there? How could we not be embarrassed by who we were last year, let alone right now? How could we not embrace the idea of a lover kindly proffering suggestions as to how we might evolve?

It's time to redefine a functioning adult. This isn't someone who bristles at the idea of change, gently suggested; it's someone who welcomes it as a path to redemption. The true adult knows they need to grow up. The truly healthy person knows they are ill (we all are). Conversely, the people who really need to change are those who think they don't need to change at all, and who say it's your problem when you float the idea. They become furious with you for even suggesting the concept and storm off, calling you weird or intense.

Of course, change has to be asked for in kindly and mature ways. We're not talking here of a bullying demand for evolution. We're talking about how much we are right to love our partners and still want them to grow up in particular ways: learn to listen more, learn to be more present, learn to be more affectionate or at least explain why they can't be, learn to get better at fathoming their own sexuality, learn to understand their past and how it affects their present, learn to defuse what makes them irrationally angry, learn to admit to their addictive behaviors and seek the help that would be on offer, learn not to humiliate us in company or betray us with friends or our children, learn how to be loyal and kind and relaxed and present and good ...

None of this is incompatible with love; it is the work of love. Love should be a classroom in which we mutually undertake to educate one another, in a spirit of support and compassion, to grow into the best versions of ourselves. Love should not be a cavern in which we endorse each other's worst sides or suffer in silence around the difficulties the other is causing us. "What would you like to change about me?" should emerge as the kindest and most mature of enquiries between partners. Rather than giving each other presents, couples should hand over the greatest gift of all, the sincerely meant question: "How can I change to make it easier for you to endure me?" That would be properly romantic.

A good enough relationship should give us the bravery to confront our flaws. "I want you to change" is not a sign of cruelty; it's proof that someone cares. The right person isn't someone without issues; it's someone who is committed to getting on top of them. Let's go even further: The natural response to being with someone who resists change, and who sees our attempts to change them as an insult, might be to wonder if it is time to make a serious change to our lives.

2
Are we just too different?

When people try to account for why certain couples break up, the emphasis typically falls on the idea of difference. A disorganized creative type was up against a managerial, ordered one; one of them liked hillwalking, while the other hated the outdoors; one was gregarious, while the other loathed parties. It seems unsurprising that they had to split.

This explanation is underpinned by a dominant theory of love: the reason why couples function is similarity; what tears them apart is difference. We get an inkling of just how widespread this theory might be when we consider the operations of modern dating sites. In their wish to help us find what they term the "right" person, they scour their databases to try to match us with someone who shares the greatest number of our tastes, interests, and attitudes. The theory is that the smaller the number of differences, the more likely the relationship is to work.

However plausible this might sound, it skirts a fundamental truth about love that we ignore at enormous cost: No couple ever breaks up because of the differences between them. They break up because one of them is fed up of not being heard. A couple might disagree on a thousand things, from the optimal frequency of sex to what kind of social life to lead, and still stay together, while another couple might be similar in almost every area, but be torn apart by a vicious sense that their competing realities are not being recognized.

What ultimately counts for the success of love is not whether there are differences, but how differences are handled—whether with curiosity, a willingness to change, mutual forgiveness, and modesty, or (in the doomed cases) with defensiveness, rigidity, and entrenchment.

We know that compatibility cannot be the basis of lasting love because, by its logic, it invariably ends up escalating absurdly. Two people who like reading, crosswords, Northern Italian cooking, ice hockey, and the music of Joni Mitchell might fall passionately in love at first, but gradually grow cross with one another as they learn that one is sympathetic to ballroom dancing, while the other wants to think more about archeology. Or one favors ragù, while the other is partial to casseroles and pies. The temptation is to resolve such frictions by abandoning all divergent partners and refining our search criteria ever more tightly. But this only forces us to seek out implausible degrees of alignment. We may end up searching for a partner who is keen on fly fishing and the novels of John le Carré but doesn't like salted butter and is good at shutting cupboard doors, or someone who loves going camping in September but who is interested in the Democratic Party (yet is also an enthusiast of tactical voting). However, of course, two such well-matched people could easily come to blows over the color of bedroom drapes, their choice of children's names, the use of napkins, or the ethics of fracking.

Pre-existing compatibility can only get us so far. At some point, even the best-matched partner will emerge as being unlike us in some way. What then matters is how the mismatch is handled. One kind of response is charming and almost aphrodisiacal in quality; the other is disappointing and, over time, insufferable.

This is what we need to hear when a conflicting perspective rears its head: "I hear you. I understand what you're saying. I am going to think about that. Perhaps I will need to change." In other words, we need to feel that our point of difference has been witnessed and, to a degree, respected. The partner may not accept our position or observation entirely, but they can see where we are coming from and are committed to examining our stance because they know that it matters to us, and they fundamentally respect our existence. They don't rush to take every uncomfortable issue off the table. In relation to gently worded complaints or criticisms, they do not immediately deny our remarks and grow enraged. They don't turn around and tell us that a problem lies entirely with us, that we're being deliberately mean, that we're the oddball, not them—and why are we complaining anyway when they've had such a hard day, and this is the last straw. They strive not to take immediate offense, get stern or fall apart—or, if they do, they apologize and try again. They are alive to the idea that they may need to evolve their position.

On the other hand, what gradually destroys love in the long term, even in the case of the most apparently well-matched couples, is an attitude of defensive pride, a shutting of the ears, a refusal to countenance that the partner may be trying to say something of desperate importance to them and has the right to be heard with a certain degree of good will and tolerance.

In the end, defensiveness is the single greatest explanation for all divorces: the inability to listen with grace to what another person is saying without resorting to stubborn pride and denial. There are no problems so grave that they make it too hard to stay; there are no differences in social attitudes or interior design tastes so severe as to doom a love affair. There are only ever terrible ways for frustrations to be expressed and heard. The lover we desperately need is not the person who shares our every taste and interest; it is the kindly soul who has learnt to negotiate differences in taste with modesty and curiosity.

3
Can people change?

"Can people change?" The question may sound somewhat abstract, as if one were asking for a friend or for the universe, but it is likely to be much more personally and painfully motivated than that.

We typically ask it when we're in a relationship with someone who is inflicting a great deal of pain on us: someone who is refusing to open their hearts or can never stop lying; someone who is aggressive or detached; someone who is harming themselves or managing to devastate us. We ask, too, because the one obvious response to frustration isn't open to us. We can't simply get up and go. We are too emotionally or practically invested to give up; something roots us to the spot. And so, with the example of one troublesome human in mind, we start to wonder about human nature in general—what it might be made of and how malleable it might be.

One thing is likely to be evident to us already: even if people can change, they don't change easily. Maybe they flare up every time we raise an issue and accuse us of being cruel or dogmatic; maybe they break down late at night and admit they have a problem, but by morning deny that anything is amiss. Maybe they say yes, they get it now, but then never deploy understanding where it really matters. At best we can conclude that by the time we've had to raise the question of change in our minds, someone around us has not managed to change either very straightforwardly or very gracefully.

We might ask a prior question: Is it okay to want someone to change? The implication from those who generate trouble for us is most often an indignant "no." But considered more imaginatively, only a perfect human would deny that they might need to grow a little in order more richly to deserve the love of another. For the rest of us, all moderately well-meaning and halfway decent requests for change should be heard with good will and, in certain cases, acted upon with immense seriousness. Those who bristle at the suggestion that they might need to change paradoxically provide the clearest evidence that they are in grave need of inner evolution.

Why might change be so hard? It isn't as if the change-resistant person is merely unsure what is amiss and will manage to alter course once an issue is pointed out—as someone might if their attention were drawn to a strand of spinach caught in their teeth. The refusal to change is more tenacious and willed than this. A person's entire character may be structured around an active aspiration not to know or feel particular things; the possibility of insight will be aggressively warded off through drink, compulsive work routines, or offended irritation with all those who attempt to spark it.

In other words, the unchanging person doesn't just lack knowledge; they are vigorously committed to not acquiring it. And they resist it because they are fleeing from something painful in their past that they were originally too weak or helpless to face and still haven't found the wherewithal to confront. We aren't so much dealing with an unchanging person as a traumatized one.

When we are on the outside, part of the problem is realizing what we are up against. The lack of change can seem frustrating because we can't apprehend why it should be so hard. Couldn't they simply move an inch or two in the right direction? But if we considered the full scale of what this person once faced, and the conditions in which their mind was formed (and certain of its doors bolted shut), we might be more realistic and more compassionate. "Couldn't they just …" would no longer quite make sense.

At the same time, very importantly, we might not stick around as long as we often do. At this juncture, perhaps we should ask ourselves a question that may feel at once unfair and rather tough: Given how clear the evidence is of a lack of change in a certain person, and hence of a lack of realistic hope that our needs are going to be met anytime soon, why are we still here? Why are we trying to open a door that can't open? Why are we returning to a recurring frustration and expecting a different result? What broken part of us can't leave a lack of fulfillment alone? What bit of our story is being re-enacted in a drama of continuously dashed hopes?

If we are talking of change, might we one day change into characters who don't sit around waiting endlessly for other people to change? Might we become better at sifting through options and allowing through only those who can already meet the lion's share of our needs? In addition, might we become better at deploying a dash of life-sustaining ruthlessness in order to leave those who tirelessly rebuff us? We may need to rebuild our minds in order to change into people who don't wonder for too long if, and when, people might change.

4
Is it worth breaking up over sex?

The most basic test of the viability of any modern relationship involves a criterion that would have sounded extremely odd to a French aristocrat in 1755, to a Scottish crofter in 1952, or indeed to most people who have existed since the emergence of our species, but that is now universally accepted and hard to overlook: an active and fulfilling sex life. It is forcefully suggested to us that it would be peculiar and, in certain ways, rather suspect to remain with anyone for any length of time if there were no intense sexual connection. Correspondingly, we could count on immediate sympathy and deep understanding if we were to announce that we had split because sex was "no longer working." If we are looking for a decent reason to leave, unsatisfactory sex seems to be all we ever need to cite.

Yet we might also recognize that there is something peculiar and perhaps a little preposterous in this stance. Would we really leave someone because of the quality or frequency of a feeling that lasts only minutes and is, from certain angles, no more or less pleasurable than a fantastic dessert or an exciting moment on the dance floor? Would we really shatter children, destroy a family, ruin assets, and put ourselves through hell for something like this? How seriously should we take the claims of sex?

Part of the reason we get confused is that sex is both a physical and an emotional phenomenon, a duality that can make it hard for us to determine the correct place it might have in our ledger of reasons to stay or to leave. There can be sex that has about as much meaning as a game of tennis and sex that seems to be a conduit to another person's soul. The act is the same, but its significance can vary beyond measure.

We might at this point venture a large claim: No one ever feels a need to leave a relationship because of "bad sex." They may say, and be inwardly convinced, that poor lovemaking is the problem, but the real issue almost certainly lies elsewhere. Equally, nonexistent or physically awkward sex can be bearable, so long as other things are in place.

What really cannot be borne, and truly is the grounds for flight, is an absence of affection. The entire point of a relationship hangs on the feeling of being witnessed, understood, accepted, stimulated, listened to, bolstered, and cherished by another person. Without this, we might as well be eating on our own for the long term. But crucially, how affection is expressed and intimated is open to a wide degree of variation. It could be done with limbs and lips, with caresses and the interplay of fantasies. But there might be other ways as well: it could be done through someone holding our hand or curling tight behind us at night, listening to our sorrows very carefully or keeping our needs closely in their minds. A light, sensitive kiss when we return home might be worth more than intercourse in terms of its ability to generate a sense of connection.

The rejection of our advances threatens to be distressing not so much because of the physical pleasures we're missing out on as because we carry within us an ongoing requirement for evidence of affection. We want to be reassured, as directly as possible, that we retain a significant place in a lover's heart. The lack of sex is not really the problem; it is the lack of closeness and tenderness it implies.

There's a huge difference between someone who is tired or not in the mood because they are preoccupied by a meeting tomorrow or a crying child in the next room, but who nevertheless understands the intensity of our longings, and a partner for whom our advances and desires are unreasonable irritants and symbols of a closeness in which they no longer have any interest. The practical result may be the same: There is no sex. But the emotional dynamics are entirely different. In the first case, we can feel loved and wanted even though (sadly) our partner can't respond. In the second case, it is very likely time to leave.

We could almost forgo the acting out of many of our desires if we knew that a partner could understand why these mattered to us and could be tender with us around the house, even if (because of their own intimate history) their relationship to the erotic ran in a different direction. Given enough affection between two people, the fact that one of them (for complex reasons) craves to perform certain physical acts—whether with their partner or with someone else—and the other one has no such appetite need not be a terminal threat. What is fatal is not that our partner can't enact our desires, but that they meet us with defensiveness, coldness, judgment, or insult.

In order to see whether a relationship might be saved, we need to accept that we may not directly be facing a sex issue, but one of underlying distance. It might theoretically be survivable if a partner never sought to have an orgasm with their companion or never fully engaged with a fantasy, so long as both parties were able to feel genuinely wanted in other ways. The distinction matters because, if we eventually split up, we need to know the real reason; if we persist in thinking the problem is a lack of sex (or not the kind of sex we want), we may misread what we are, in essence, seeking from another person. We are not after the perfect sexual partner; we're after something yet more critical and often harder to secure: a good enough source of affection and understanding. We might, in another but better relationship, end up having the same rather negligible quantity of sex, but no longer resent the paucity because we have found a raft of other, and in many ways more stable, ways of feeling assured of another's love.

5
What about the children?

For most of human history, people didn't stay in relationships for love. They stayed in them in order to protect their assets, ensure their status, pool their resources, synchronize farming implements, and guarantee the welfare of their children. It is only in the last few minutes of our evolution (250 years at most) that we have conducted our relationships under a very different ideology: that of a movement of ideas known as Romanticism. For Romanticism, the most important aspect of any relationship is not practical; it is the emotional intensity that connects a couple: how good the sex is, how much we feel understood, and to what degree a partner feels like a soulmate.

This hugely ambitious and distinctive philosophy of love has created a very large puzzle around what was, traditionally, an obvious priority for any couple: keeping a child under one roof with his or her own parents. From the dawn of settled agricultural societies, a high degree of family unity was understood to take precedence over the inner satisfaction and emotional buoyancy of the parents. That a husband might be quietly weeping because of his wife's emotional distance, or that a wife might be stifling her yawns at her husband's repetitive conversation would have been considered unfortunate, no doubt, but not matters over which a person would have any desire or, indeed, opportunity to run away and begin life anew. Couples stayed together not because each thought highly of the other, but because they were bound together by forbidding practical, status, and religious obligations. It didn't matter a jot whether they happened to be lyrically happy or on the edge of terminal despair.

This was brutal at points, but arguably had certain upsides, or at least a certain clarity as far as children were concerned. Their parents were not going to split up merely because they couldn't align their aesthetic tastes or rarely tried out new sexual positions. And children weren't going to shuttle from one household to another and have a bevy of stepbrothers and sisters just because, a few years back, one parent started to feel rejected when the other became unresponsive to their night-time caresses.

Nowadays, however, any partner wounded by the collapse of the emotional bond with their partner is automatically faced with a momentous choice: should they leave for the sake of their own heart, or should they stay for the sake of the children?

A dominant theory has often sought to extend the concerns of Romanticism into the realm of children. According to this interpretation, children, too, care a lot about the authenticity of their parents' bond. They think a lot about, and are exercised by, the emotional honesty circulating between partners. Like their elders, they also want love to be "true." As a result, advice is often given that couples should separate in order to demonstrate to their children the wisdom of an emotion-centric Romantic existence. It is better for children to have (for example) two bedrooms and four step-siblings and know that their parents are now properly fulfilled and in love.

It makes a lot of sense, and in many cases must surely be the right answer. But it is worth considering an alternative view that begins in a different place: with a contrasting analysis of what children might really want.

In this philosophy, children are conceived of as essentially practical creatures, comparable in many ways to guests who have decided to spend their holidays in a particular hotel under a certain management, whom they've grown very used to and (usually) very fond of. What these guests want above all is to secure a set of pragmatic and understandable goals:

–   They want the least administrative hassle.
–   They want the adults around them to get on cheerfully.
–   They want as little alteration in routine as possible.
–   They don't want to be made to hang out with new people.

- They don't want to meet a half-naked adult
  stranger at breakfast.
- They don't want rumors to circulate about their
  "hotel" that might make them look weird in front
  of their peers.

That said, they arguably don't particularly care
about a whole host of other things:

- They don't care how often, or how pleasingly,
  their parents are having sex.
- They don't care whether their parents are the
  deepest sorts of soulmates.
- They don't care what their parents get up to in
  their spare time.

These comparative lists start to suggest a possible
answer to the dilemma of whether a person might stay
or leave in so far as the welfare of children is the issue.
The question can be answered either way. Both staying
and leaving could be made compatible with children's
concerns, because the emotional satisfaction of their
parents is not the central issue for young people. The
central issue is how much disruption there might be
in their lives. There are ways of staying that will cause
massive disruptions: horrific fights between the hotel
managers that won't allow the guests to enjoy their

time, for example. And there are ways of leaving that also create extreme disruption, or that stir up almost no disruption. The reason the stay-or-leave question is so tricky is that children don't really care whether you stay or leave; they want an undisturbed life, a pleasant atmosphere, and a good mood among the management, which could be compatible or incompatible with either choice. It just depends how it's done.

For those who might want to leave, we can imagine conceiving of a range of innovations:

- Perhaps the children wouldn't move between homes; instead the parents would.
- Perhaps the children wouldn't hang out much with new partners, just the parents would.
- Perhaps the children wouldn't have to know about the depths of the disappointment between the parents; they'd just notice a sensible and kindly relationship between them.

A concern for more authentic and emotionally alive relationships has been, in many ways, an enormous advance for humanity. But it has left us very confused as to what the priorities are for children. A non-Romantic worldview provides a clear answer: We don't need to spend the rest of our life with someone with whom we no longer connect "for the sake of the children." But at the same time, we must ensure that if we leave, everything is done to keep the practical basis of a child's life as stable as possible—as with a hotel that has come under new, divided ownership, but bends over backward to make sure its guests suffer few inconveniences.

Our own emotional maelstrom is deeply consuming. One day, our offspring may have something similar going on in their lives, but for now, as children, they are blessedly down-to-earth creatures. They want to know that no one is at anyone's throat, that breakfast is going to be at the same time and place it's always been, and that they don't have to become instant friends with a bunch of new guests they're not in the mood for. Those should be our priorities as parents; all the other stuff is, in the nicest way, our business alone and should remain as much until the day, which might never come, when the now grown-up guest takes an interest in what the hotel management was really going through all those years ago.

6
Have we tried everything?

One of the preconditions of a successful ending to any relationship is a secure sense that we have "tried everything" before closing the door behind us. Only once we are reasonably certain that we have exhausted all options can a departure start to feel considered and therefore warranted. The greatest hedge against regret is effort.

Among the effortful options, few can be as grueling but also as vital as the business of couples therapy. We might go so far as to propose that no relationship should ever be considered doomed until a couple has tried out no less but also not much more than nine months of couples therapy.

Like many things that help relationships, couples therapy can sound deeply unromantic, involving visits to a usually drab consulting room, where we must face a host of embarrassing conversations about matters that it would be much nicer never to have to think about, let alone discuss with a partner and a trained stranger.

Our culture teaches us to trust and follow our feelings in love. But couples therapy knows this to be highly problematic, for our feelings are frequently erroneous and encoded with primitive responses from the troublesome past. Instead, it encourages us to stand back from our instincts, to neutralize them through understanding and, where possible, to reroute them in less self-punishing, less impatient, and more trusting directions. Living alongside another person is one of the hardest things we can ever attempt; couples therapy knows this, and so it suggests that we should expect to get it wrong unaided and feel unashamed about the need for in-depth training.

There are a number of vital things we might learn in our months in therapy. For a start, in a quiet room, we finally have the chance to define what we feel the problems in the relationship really are, without things degenerating into shouting, sulking, or avoidance. We're normally far too cross with, or upset by, our partner to be able to share with them, in a way they might understand, what we're angry and upset with them about. It helps to be in front of a stranger we're both a little intimidated by and with whom we have to behave ourselves. It is highly unusual to be able to put things so starkly, but also so reasonably: "That you never touch me and behave so limply and unenthusiastically when I touch you is slowly killing me—and though I love you, I don't know how much longer I can take it." How much better to voice something like this than to go through a decade of low-level sniping and repressed fury.

Secondly, therapists are skilled at teasing out from us why what bothers us bothers us. Normally, left to our own devices, we don't unearth the emotional meaning behind our positions. We squabble about where to go on the weekend, rather than explaining what going out or staying in represents for us internally. As a result, the other finds us merely stubborn and mean, and all that is interesting and poignant in our position is lost.

Thirdly, therapists break up unseen, repeated patterns of upset and retaliation. A classic therapeutic game is to ask both parties to fill in the blanks:

When you ... I feel ... and I respond by ...

So: "When you disregard the children, I feel rejected and then respond by trying to control whom you see in the evenings." Or: "When you don't touch me in bed, I feel invisible and respond by being ungrateful about your money."

With the therapist acting as an honest broker, new contracts can be drawn up, along the lines of: "If you do x, I will do y." Once we get a little bit of what we really want (but usually haven't properly asked for), the other's needs feel a lot less onerous and hateful.

Sometimes the advice is almost beautifully pedantic. Name three things you resent about your partner. And, next, three things you deeply appreciate. Keep the criticism specific: not "you're cold and ungrateful," but "if you can call me when you're running late, then ..."

Families can be kept intact with as little as this.

Through therapy, we are challenged to abandon some of our grimmer ideas about how people can be and what will happen to us in love: "If I am vulnerable, I am not necessarily going to be hurt," or "I might try to explain, and the other could listen." We are given the security to throw out some of the scripts we grew up with about the futility of ever trying to be understood. We can start to be moved by one another's pain. "What does it feel like," a good therapist will ask, "to hear your partner explain how it is for them when you …?" We can start to take care of each other. A remarkable idea comes to the fore: that our partner isn't really our enemy, that they— like us—have some very bad ways of getting across what are some very understandable and touching needs.

Couples therapy is a classroom where we can learn how to love. We're normally so embarrassed by not having the first clue how to do that so we leave things until we are too angry or despairing to do anything but hate. The most hopeful and therefore romantic thing we can ever do in relationships is sometimes to declare that we haven't yet learnt how to love—but, with a little help, are keen to learn one day.

Of course, all this may not work. The partner might not listen as we had hoped, and vice versa. In the cold light of the consulting room, we might come to see them as intransigent and not worthy of our care. Our exchanges, far from advancing understanding, might serve to reveal just how unable we are to make any sense to one another. Far from rescuing the relationship, couples therapy might conclusively bury it.

However, this need not be an argument against therapy. A failed course at least provides us with useful proof of why things had to end. It may not have saved love, but it will have done something almost as valuable: made us a little less sad, and a little more sure, that it has died.

7
What if I end up lonely?

In the privacy of our minds, one shameful thought may haunt us as we evaluate whether to stay in or get out of an unsatisfactory relationship: What if we were to leave and end up in a place of terrible loneliness?

We're meant to be above such pragmatic worries. Only cowards and reprobates would mind a few weekends (or decades) by themselves. We've heard of those books that sing the praises of solitude (the divorcee who relocated to a solitary hut on a bare Scottish island; the person who went sailing around the world in a dinghy). But we can admit that we're not naturals at this sort of thing. There have been empty days when we almost lost our minds. There was one trip that we took on our own years back that was, behind the scenes, a psychological catastrophe. We're not really in a position to wave away the dangers of being left alone on a rock.

Without wishing to play down the dangers, there are one or two things we might learn to weaken our fears and thereby come to a clearer view of whether to stay or leave. We can begin with a simple observation: It is typically a lot worse to be on our own on a Saturday than on a Monday night, and a lot worse to be alone over the festive period than at the end of the tax year. The physical reality and the length of time we're by ourselves may be identical, but the feeling that comes with being so is entirely different. This apparently negligible observation holds out a clue for a substantial solution to loneliness.

The difference between the Saturday and the Monday night comes down to the contrast between what being alone appears to mean on the two respective dates. On a Monday night, our own company feels as if it brings no judgment in its wake; it doesn't depart from the norms of respectable society; it's what's expected of decent people at the start of a busy week. We get back from work, make some soup, catch up on the post, do some emails and order a few groceries, without any sense of being unusual or cursed. The next day, when a colleague asks us what we got up to, we can relate the truth without any hot prickles of shame. It was just a Monday night, after all. But Saturday night finds us in a far more perilous psychological zone. We scan our phone for any sign of a last-minute invitation; we flick through the channels in an impatient and disconsolate haze; we are alive to our own tragedy as we eat tuna from a can; we take a long bath at 8.30 p.m. to try to numb the discomfort inside with scalding heat on the outside; and as we prepare to turn out the light just after ten, the high-spirited cries of revelers walking by our house seem to convey a targeted tone of mockery and pity. On Monday morning, we pass over the whole horrid incident with haste.

From this, we conclude that being alone is bearable in relation to how "normal" (that nebulous yet influential concept) the condition feels to us; it can either be a break from an honorably busy life, or sure evidence that we are an unwanted, wretched, disgusting, and emotionally diseased being.

This is tricky but ultimately hopeful, for it suggests that if we could work on what being alone means to us, we could theoretically end up as comfortable in our own skin on a long summer Saturday night filled with the joyous cries of our fellow citizens as on the dreariest Monday in November. We could spend the whole holiday season by ourselves feeling as relaxed and as unselfconscious as we did when we were children and hung out for days by ourselves, tinkering with a project on our bedroom floor, with no thought that anyone would think us sad or shameful. We may not after all need a new companion (something that can be hard to find in a panic); we just need a new mindset (which we can take care of by ourselves, starting right now).

To build ourselves a new mental model of what being alone should truly mean, we might rehearse a few of the following arguments:

i.

Our solitude is willed

Despite what an unfriendly voice inside our heads might tell us, we are the ones who can choose whether or not to be alone. Assuming it's the latter, we could if we wanted to be in all sorts of company. Our solitude is willed rather than imposed. No one ever needs to be alone so long as they don't mind who they are with.

But we do mind, and we may have good reasons to do so. The wrong kind of company is much lonelier for us than being by ourselves—that is, it's further from what matters to us, more grating in its insincerity and more of a reminder of disconnection and misunderstanding than is the conversation we can have in the quiet of our own minds. Being alone is not proof that we have been rejected by the world; it's evidence that we've taken a good look at the available options and have—with wisdom—done some rejecting ourselves.

ii.

Beware outward signs of companionship

It seems, from a distance, as if everyone is having an ecstatic time. The party (what we imagine in our darkest moments to be the unitary joyous social event from which we've been blocked) grips our imaginations. We've passed the restaurants and seen the groups leaning back in their chairs and laughing uproariously; we've seen the couples holding hands and the families packing up for their glorious vacations abroad. We know the depths of fun that are unfolding.

But we need to hold on to what we recognize in our sober moments is a more complicated reality: that there is going to be alienation at the restaurant, bitterness between the couples, and despair in the sunny island hotels. We picture intimacy and communion, deep understanding, and the most sophisticated varieties of kindness. We are sure that "everyone" is having precisely what we understand by true love. But they are not. They will, for the most part, be together but still alone; they will be talking but largely not heard.

Isolation and grief are not unique to us; they are a fundamental part of the human experience. They trail every member of our species, whether in a couple or alone. We've chosen to experience the pains of existence by ourselves for now, but having a partner has never protected anyone from the void for very long. We should take care to drown our individual sorrows in the ocean of a redemptive and darkly funny universal pessimism. No one is particularly enjoying the journey; we are not built that way. As we should never allow ourselves to forget in front of steamed-up restaurant windows, life is suffering for most of us for most of the time.

iii.
We get statistics wrong

To compound our errors, we are the most hopeless statisticians. We should pin a notice to our kitchen wall reminding us of this. We say that "everyone" is happy and "everyone" is in a couple. But we need to properly evaluate what is going on in a statistical sense.

We are letting self-disgust, not mathematics, decide our vision of "normality." If we really surveyed the question, if we grew wings and went up and examined the city, swooping in on this bedroom here and that office there, those families in the park and that couple on a date, we'd see something altogether different. We'd see millions of others like us and far worse: this one crying over a letter, that one shouting that they've had enough, this one complaining that they can't be understood, that one weeping in the bathroom over an argument. It is regrettable enough to be sad; we don't need to compound the misery by telling ourselves—through a grave misunderstanding of statistics—that it is abnormal to be so.

iv.

There is nothing shameful in what we're doing

Our images of being alone lack dignity. We need better role models. Those on their own aren't always the cobwebbed figures of our nightmares. Some of the greatest people who have ever lived have chosen, for a variety of noble reasons, to spend a lot of time by themselves. Out of self-compassion, we need to keep the difference between enforced and willed solitude firmly in consciousness. Here is a world-renowned scientist spending twenty years on their own to finish a book that will change everything. Here is one of the most beautiful people nature has yet produced, alone in their room, playing the piano, because their own company feels more peaceful than that of a jealous ex. Here is a politician who once led the nation, now preferring to commune with others through books. Those who are by themselves don't comprise only the desperate cases; they number many of those we would feel most privileged to meet.

v.

Understand your past

The sense of shame you experience at being in your own company normally comes from somewhere very particular: your own childhood, and, in particular, from an unlovable vision of yourself that you picked up in the early years. Somewhere in the past, someone left you feeling unworthy. Now, whenever you suffer a reversal, the story is ready to re-emerge, confirming what you think is a fundamental truth about you: that you don't deserve to exist. It's not essentially that you're afraid of being lonely; it's that you don't like yourself very much. The cure for this is immense sympathy and psychotherapeutic understanding, but not, perhaps, the company of a partner you no longer care for or respect.

* * *

Once we can like ourselves more, we won't need to be so scared of friendship with ourselves; we will know that others aren't laughing at us cruelly and that there is no delightful party we've been barred from. We'll appreciate that we can be both on our own and a fully dignified, legitimate member of the human race. We'll have conquered the terror of loneliness—and therefore, at last, we'll be in a position to assess our options correctly, without fear, and to choose freely whether to stay in or leave the relationship we're in.

8
What if I just repeat the same mistakes?

As we ponder leaving a relationship, we might be stopped by an unfamiliar and perturbing thought: What if we were somewhat to blame as well? Naturally, "they" are chiefly always at fault; it's really the only way to sleep. But a primordial honesty may force us to wonder whether blame can be so neatly apportioned. What if there was something we did to make our relationship harder than it needed to be? What if we were somehow psychologically very troublesome? And what if we left at tremendous cost but ignorant of ourselves, and then ended up in exactly the same place with somebody else in a few months or years?

These may be about the most fruitful worries we can ever hope to have. Indeed, we really shouldn't be deemed safe to leave until we've started to wonder in depth about how dangerous we might be around other people.

The true tragedy of relationships is not that they go wrong, but that we learn so little from them when they do. In a better future society, ending relationships should be rendered simple at the practical level; marriages should be concluded without any of the current costs and bureaucratic delays. But only on one condition: that both parties would be able to show an advanced understanding of why their relationship had failed; what it was about them individually and as a couple that made their union so hard. We would need to pass an exit exam—and for a very simple and humane reason: that only when two people, who will presumably soon be dating again, have grasped why they might be difficult for someone else emotionally will the rest of the public be adequately protected from the huge risks posed by ongoing self-ignorance. The exit exam would not be a punitive measure, just a basic instrument of public health.

The essential truth about relationships is that the way we love as adults has a history. The candidates we choose and our characteristic way of dealing with them and conceiving of their motives mirrors expectations formed around our earliest caregivers. We cannot understand the fate of any single relationship without threading it into the dynamics we knew at the beginning of our lives. As grown-ups we don't find love so much as embark on a quest to refind it, striving with varying degrees of self-awareness to recreate with our partners many of the patterns and emotions we first experienced around parental figures.

If our adult love lives tend to be so difficult, then it is because the love we tasted in childhood will, in many cases, not have been straightforward. There might have been affection and kindness, but these are likely to have come wrapped up with more troubling and painful emotions: a feeling of never being good enough; a sense that we needed to protect someone from certain truths about ourselves; a fear of abandonment or a rage we had to appease. We find ourselves gravitating toward people not, first and foremost, on the basis that they are good or kind to us, but because they feel familiar. With them, we re-experience affection and gentleness, but also, at times, an impression of not measuring up to expectations or of being shut out or ignored. It may not be fun, yet it feels right. We may reject healthier candidates not because we don't, on paper, recognize their virtues, but because (as we can't ever quite admit) we sense that they won't make us suffer in the ways we have to suffer in order to feel that we are properly in love.

More tragically still, not only do we sometimes refind unhealthy partners, we have a propensity to imagine we have done so even when we haven't. Someone with a difficult past may permanently suspect that even quite innocent candidates are about to treat them in the same way as the damaging figures who let them down in childhood. Although this may be false, they will at every turn feel as if they are reencountering the mother who humiliated them or the father who ignored them— and will, as a result, behave with a degree of instinctive defensiveness or untrusting aggression that is wholly unwarranted and may, in the end, exhaust the patience of even the most initially willing partner.

A functioning exit exam would ideally start to tease out all this. Here would be some of the key questions a candidate would face:

1.   What was unsatisfactory or painful in your relationship with your parent of the gender you're attracted to?

2.   How have the difficulties above tended to show up in your adult relationships? Do you notice repetitions?

3.   Alternatively, have you been so keen to get away from childhood dynamics that you have denied yourself some of the good qualities that existed, alongside the troubling ones, in your original caregivers? Do you keep running into difficulties because you can be attracted only to people who are in no way (for example) intelligent or punctual, successful or sweet-natured, because these qualities evoke something too painful that you are in flight from in your earlier life?

4.   What awful or painful thing do you suspect a partner may do to you? And what, in your fear that they may hurt you, do you do to or around them that is less than productive? How fair is the fear?

5.   What did you learn about communication in childhood? How good are you at sharing the more wounded, sad, or emotionally vulnerable parts of yourself?

6.   Complete the sentence: "When I am hurt, I tend to ..." Complete the sentence: "Rather than explain clearly and calmly what is wrong, I ..." Complete the sentence: "I jump to conclusions around ..."

7.   In so far as you have a tendency to pick partners who mirror past problems, to save time on future dates, what is the earliest possible sign that would indicate that you had found someone with whom you would end up in a familiar, frustrating place? Knowing what you know now, what would have been the first warning signs that your perhaps soon-to-be ex was going to prove challenging? What do you vow to look out for and run away from more successfully next time?

8.   We may not always have the option to change our types, but we do have the option to change how we characteristically respond to these types. Currently we often respond according to a script from early childhood. We behave with great immaturity: we sulk, we nag, we get defensive or furious. But there is always a chance of responding in a more mature way (by explaining, not

blaming ourselves excessively, avoiding rage, etc.), which may be enough to transform the fate of a relationship. How could you—now or in the future—behave in more obviously adult ways in relation to the difficulties that arise with the kinds of people you are drawn to?

9.   If you were able to pick a different sort of partner next time, what would they be like? How could you be sure that they were not the same thing beneath a surface difference?

10.   You may have spent a long time not leaving this relationship, despite knowing it was wrong. What in your past can explain this propensity to get stuck? What might you tell yourself in order to be more decisive and less compliant next time?

A relationship may be over; there is a failure of sorts in that brute fact. But the end need not prove disastrous to either party in the long term, so long as sufficient insight can be pulled from the ashes. The least we can do to atone for the hurt we experience and cause in unhappy love stories is to make sure that we can—at a minimum— point to one or two things we have learnt that will make us a bit less dangerous next time.

9
Can I cope practically?

When it comes to relationships, the age we live in has a firm belief in distributing practical tasks equally. Both parties are meant to display comparable competence at, and enthusiasm for, earning money and managing household chores. It is not acceptable to complain that buying dishwasher tablets or spending the day in an office might ultimately not be "our thing."

Nevertheless, beneath the radar, a lot of relationships show considerable variation from the official ideology. In private, there are many couples where someone is doing very little of the earning and/or very little of the ironing or dentist appointment scheduling.

This problem has nothing to do with politics and everything to do with what may occur when the relationship starts to experience a serious breakdown in intimacy and connection. At this point, this dimension risks emerging as the single greatest contributor to a feeling of stuckness and entrapment. Honesty may force us to admit that—however humiliating this might sound—we are unable to leave a union not because we don't know our own hearts or still have hope that communication might improve, but because we wouldn't have the remotest clue how to pay a tax bill, call up a plumber, or refill the car with windscreen wiper fluid. We stay not because we are still in love, but because we are terrified of laundry.

Although the problem of helplessness tends to manifest itself in the head of one party, it is really both members of the couple who are responsible for its creation—and, as ever, the past explains most of the dynamics.

In their early years, all children require two kinds of love: practical love on the one hand and emotional love on the other. They need to have their clothes changed, their shoelaces tied, their meals cooked, their homework interpreted, and their hair combed, but they also need to be cuddled, held, heard, sung to, played with, and cherished.

Unfortunately, it can be difficult to find the right balance between practical and emotional love. There are cases where a parent may find it easier to take care of the practical than the emotional dimensions of a relationship with a child. They may love their child deeply, but not be able to convey their love freely in an emotional key. They may limit their role to ensuring that the child will always have new shoes for school and never develop a cavity. At an extreme, the parent may require the practical weakness or cluelessness of their child in order to bolster their own sense of worth. Sensing the parent's limitations, the child may then unconsciously collude in giving the adult as much opportunity as possible to express their concern and aptitude. They will become helpless to ensure that an adult they love will have a role. They can't do very much around the house; they lose all their schoolbooks (and the parent is wonderful at finding them again); they love the parent's food but wouldn't have the first clue how to fry an egg; they often fall ill and need someone to bring them medicine and tea. To reject any of the parent's help would (the child instinctively grasps) be to deliver a cruel blow to their identity. In a way, it works for both parties, though at considerable internal cost.

The danger is that these exaggerated patterns are then repeated in adult love. Here, too, we may find a partner who shuns some of the rawness and exposure demanded of emotional love in favor of immense devotion to practical tasks. Almost without being asked, they may start buying their partner all their clothes or taking on any job that comes up around the house; they may monopolize every aspect of the finances or take over the management of the kitchen. This absorption of the practical realm may also feel compelling to their partner, who, because of their own historic association between love and practical care, will gratefully acquiesce to ever more assistance, growing increasingly incompetent and dependent in the process, until they genuinely believe themselves unable to put on a wool wash or earn a payslip.

On both sides, a challenge is being avoided: for the helper, the challenge of betting that they can be loved by someone not because they have rearranged their sock drawer or paid for lunch, but because they are worthy of being honored and appreciated for their own essential emotional self. And for the helpless dependent, the challenge is believing that they can enjoy a love based not on practical care, but on a fulfilling emotional and sexual connection with an equal.

In order to exit a stuck relationship (and prise ourselves free from the potential for repetition), we may need to disentangle and remake more accurately an association that may have built up in our minds between practical and emotional love. We need to have the courage to stop manically looking after people in a material sense as an alternative to allowing ourselves to experience the vagaries, exposures, and joys of a psychologically mutual relationship. We need to stop colluding in our own infantilization and trust that we are as capable as the next person of taking the trash out and calling the dentist.

We may need to leave—or perhaps should try to stay. But we will never know which it is until we have purged the relationship of the unhealthy choreography of helpless child on the one hand and super-practical adult on the other. We'll be in a position to assess our real options when we have done the easy bit—figured out how to earn some money and clean the oven—and moved on to the real hurdle: allowing ourselves to need, to be vulnerable around and to trust an equal.

10
Who is rejecting whom?

When a relationship ends, we expect it to be fairly easy to determine who ended it and who wished it to continue. The person who said they wanted out, who explicitly called for the breakup, who bought a new apartment and who might be on the search for a new partner is evidently the one who ended things; and the one who proposed remaining together, who argued for giving it another shot and who said loudly that they had no wish to break up is just as evidently the one who remained loyal.

But this may be a naïve and unwittingly cruel view of how relationships can end. In reality, it isn't necessarily the one who leaves who is doing the rejecting, nor the one who ostensibly seeks to remain who is the one being rejected. Not everyone who leaves hates, and not everyone who stays loves. The person who really "leaves" is the one who withdraws affection. And the one who really "remains" is the one who believes in closeness with a partner, even if the frustration of this belief can end up causing this person to quit.

Beneath the distinction between leaving and staying lies a more important distinction: between love and indifference. Although one could imagine that leaving would go with indifference and staying would go with love, there are cases where a person seeks to keep a relationship going and yet acts in a subtly indifferent or covertly hostile manner toward their partner. They may clearly claim that they don't want things to end. But to the profound puzzlement of the partner, their day-to-day behavior expresses something rather different; their manner may be distant, their caresses few, their physical attentions negligible.

This doublespeak can drive the partner to extreme confusion and even the brink of a breakdown, for they will be told that what they long for is available even as the practical evidence points to the contrary. There is always a reason why it's too late for sex or a hand isn't there to hold—but to complain is invariably to meet with anger and denial or promises of a brighter future next time. Not only is the partner being neglected, they are made to feel insane for suggesting they might be so.

Eventually, worn down by the dissonance between word and deed, the emotionally ignored party may lose their patience and declare that they are off, not because they truly want to be, but because they've been forced to conclude that their partner will never be able to assuage their needs. They are leaving not because they don't love, but because the love they have to give doesn't feel as if it will ever be answered.

It is a particular burden when a person not only has to bear the sadness of being turned down, but also has to carry the guilt of having ended the relationship in the face of a host of protestations of loyalty by their covertly cold partner. To spare themselves the ravages of self-hatred, the departing lover should daily rehearse in their mind how they got to this place. As they head for the door, their truth is not "I am leaving you because I hate you," but "I am leaving you because I love you so much and have tried so hard, too hard, to elicit a matching love that never felt available."

Such an awareness won't dull the pain, but it will repatriate emotions and lessen an unfair burden of responsibility. One is leaving, perhaps, but one simultaneously deserves all the sympathy and compassion due to someone who has, at heart, been gruesomely—and surreptitiously—rejected.

11
Why do I continue to
feel so stuck?

This is for those among us who continue to feel secretly stuck. We may feel very drawn to staying, occasionally tempted to leave and unable to resolve the dilemma one way or the other. We alternate between periods in which we manage to convince ourselves that it might, after all, be bearable and recurring crises when we acknowledge that we are—by remaining—well on the way to ruining the one life we will ever be granted. Torn between intense shame and untenable claustrophobia, weak in the face of our conundrum, we may start to fantasize that someone or something else—a parent, the government, a war, an illness, a divine command—might magically resolve the problem for us; like desperate children, we hope against hope that something might just show up.

But because it behoves everyone eventually—and with nothing unkind being meant by this—to try to become an adult (that is, a person who can alter their circumstances through their own agency), we may benefit from a few ideas to strengthen our resolve.

For a start, we are here not because we are evil, fickle, or unlucky, but because we probably had a challenging childhood. This could sound like an odd idea to bring up, but the matter does appear evident in structure, however impossible the repercussions can feel in practice. Anyone can end up in an unhappy relationship. But those who get badly stuck in them, those who cannot find the courage to have a difficult conversation and move on, those who spend years feeling intensely ashamed of what they want and doubting their right to aim for anything more satisfying, these creatures are a particular subcategory of humans.

They are the ones who, when they were little, probably never learnt the art of confident self-assertion; they are liable to be creatures who never felt they had much right to tell others what they needed and to stick up for their vision of contentment, whatever the short-term troubles that might ensue. We, the stuck ones, were the good children, the under-loved ones, the ones who were scared of angry parents or overly anxious about fragile ones. We are the ones who, too early on, learnt to comply and obey, to worry about everyone else, to fit in and to smile. Now, decades later, we are the ones who cannot get up and leave because we would, at some level, rather die than make a fuss.

But however appealing that can sound, there's a small part of us that won't let us die like this; a part of us that awkwardly refuses to shut up and be stifled; a healthy part of us that won't let us continue without the kind of love we crave; a part of us that is like a germinating seed with strength enough to move aside a one-tonne concrete slab in order to reach the light.

We endlessly question the legitimacy of our aspirations. Is it fair to want what we want? Is it normal to seek whatever it is that's currently missing: more love, more intellectual stimulation, more friendship, more sex, more solemnity, more laughs? We would, in a way, love someone to tell us that we were plainly wrong. But the reality is that there can never be an objective measure in these matters. We want what we want and no amount of arguing with ourselves can make our appetites go away or delegitimize our needs. The way forward is not to call ourselves difficult and shut up but to learn to honor and adroitly defend our own inner complexity.

Stuck people are agonized to the point of paralysis by the prospect of causing difficulties; they possibly already have a lot of hesitation about asking strangers where the bathroom is. So now they worry whether their partner would ever recover, what friends would say, or how the family would deal with it. The last thing that occurs to them is how much, in the end, everyone copes. The frightening yet liberating truth is how little anyone actually cares. Even the hurt lover will recover and come to appreciate the benefits of freedom as opposed to enduring a constant emotional tourniquet around their heart. An orderly life is a fine and beautiful thing, but it can only ever be so when it sits on top of a flourishing relationship, rather than when it is fostered as a substitute for one. Better to blow up a home than to continue in one unworthy of the name.

The way to start getting unstuck is via a strange-sounding move: by valuing ourselves more. We must accept that the point of a relationship is not to suffer, that some things are necessary but fewer than we think— and that no one will congratulate us on our deathbeds for having thrown away our lives. We are not suffering because we need to, but because we have grown up to be people for whom suffering feels horribly and compellingly familiar. We may need to take the entirely unknown step of telling the world what we truly want.

12
Why are they so puzzling?

Breakups are almost invariably difficult, but there are different degrees of complexity at stake in different situations. Nor does this deny the existence of a cataclysmically painful but too-little-known type whom we can call the hardest person in the world to break up with.

A relationship with them begins like this: you're very drawn to them. Perhaps they very much attract you physically and their personality is compelling as well. You admire them and, in areas, feel a lot of sympathy for them too. There's probably something in their past that really interests and touches you. You have no desire to break up and, in fact, you'd love this to last till the end.

For their part, they seem to be keen on you. That's what they've said a number of times. They show no interest in leaving you. They want this to be for the long term, perhaps forever.

But there is a problem—one so grave and yet so hidden, so damaging and yet so hard to grasp, that you can only bear to face up to it slowly. You start to realize that the partner whom you love and who says they love you is having a grievously detrimental effect on your mental well-being.

What wrong might the partner be perpetrating? It is a spectrum. At one end, they might be hitting you. But the spectrum is long, and it contains all sorts of insidious ways in which, without ever raising a hand, let alone a finger, one human can badly damage another. They might be having affairs or spending too much money. They might be addicted to something. Or—and this is hard to get a grip on—they may be constantly "absent." They show no reliable warmth toward you; they never initiate any touch; they may never hug. They are present but not really there.

Probably, as soon as these problems first arose, you started to complain. But you did so softly, or sarcastically, or bitterly—not head on. After all, you love them and you're a good boy or girl. It can take a long time—years or decades—before you are able to raise an adult objection. What happens when you at last ask these types to face up to the harm you feel they are doing to you? There are two main responses; both are hard to master, but the second is the hardest.

i.
They confess it

Fed up at last, you tell them that you've had enough of the violence, affairs, addiction, financial spend, distance, lack of intimacy, lack of sex … You raise an ultimatum.

If they don't finally raise their game, you're going to leave (even though, of course, it's the last thing you want—you love them!).

You may be shaking and flushed after you have spoken. You feel you might be crazy (surely it's crazy to threaten to leave someone you love and who says they love you). You'd expected all sorts of dark responses on their part, but something that is, on the surface, rather lovely now happens. They admit it. They confess. They say: "You're right. I hadn't fully realized until now, until you finally opened my eyes to how I've harmed you. Baby, I hear you. I'm so sorry!"

The person promises that they will change. They just need time; they just need your understanding. They suggest getting themselves a therapist, once a month or so, and then they'll get on top of their issues. Their candor is moving and suggests they have a handle on their psyche. You are, in any case, desperate to believe them; they have a very receptive audience.

The problem is that, despite their promises, the person doesn't change. They make a short-term adjustment, enough to ensure you won't leave them on the timescale you were threatening, but not profound enough to correct the problem—and allow you your freedom.

And in the gap between their promise to change and your realization that they don't have the ability (or perhaps intention) to do so, children may have been born (they wanted kids to keep you around; you wanted them as a token of the happy future that was being promised). Commitments pile up and there are fewer options left in the world beyond. You might not be so young anymore.

ii.
They deny it

However hideous all the above sounds, there is an even worse kind of relationship to leave than that. This is one with the same dynamics, but with one extra twist at the end. When you finally confront them with the problem, they don't confess; they deny it. They tell you you're dreaming, you're imagining it, that the problem lies with you. They become incensed and offended at the suggestion you're making: "You're so cynical about me. Don't you trust me? How rude you are about me! Why don't you have more faith in me and in us?" They push back: "You're just as neurotic as you say I am. The problem is with you and not me …"

This is minefield territory. Relationships and their interactions are generally not filmed, so it's hard for you to back up your claims, or even to be sure of your verdicts, when they are relentlessly challenged. Is the loved one spending too much money or am I just nagging? Are they actually flirting or am I just jealous? Are they failing to initiate sex or am I just insecure?

The partner whom you love and really don't want to leave and who says they love you adds to the difficulty by telling you, with authority, that you really are crazy, that you are seeing things, that you are too demanding, that there's something wrong with you …

Probably, you're an open-minded, nice, intelligent person—and open-minded, nice, intelligent people tend to give others the benefit of the doubt. After all, such types know they aren't perfect; they're aware of everything they get wrong; they don't feel they're brilliant in every way. Therefore, perhaps it's plausible that here, too, you may be seeing things that aren't there—so why insist, especially when you love your partner and want to be with them? Here is a nice person telling you that you are a bit mad and imagining things. It's a dispiriting message, but if disregarding your impulses (and your emotional needs) is the price you pay for keeping a relationship afloat, maybe it's worth thinking of yourself as a bit insane. At least you'll still have a partner.

So more time passes and you stay put. In that time, probably there are more children, more entanglements, and less of life left for you to build on afterward. There is also likely to be a destruction of your sense of reality. You will probably start to feel as mad as you're being subtly told you are. You might have a breakdown, which is not an ideal backdrop against which to leave anyone.

* * *

All that said, in both of the above cases, you will probably have to leave eventually. Your long-term mental well-being may depend on it. But it is no picnic, having to leave someone you love, who says they love you—and who is either falsely promising to change or denying they need to change because you're the defective one.

In order to leave, you will need to think: "I am in love with someone who is damaged. They cannot realistically change and may even be using me as a reason not to change. Or they are in denial and are abusing my credulity and self-doubt in order not to look more honestly into themselves." You will have to think: "There is probably something in my past, a history of putting up with intolerable situations, that makes me a long-term sucker for this sort of suffering."

Mountain climbers know that certain peaks cannot be climbed alone. You need a climbing buddy. In this context, let's call them a psychotherapist or a very good friend. They can put in the time to reassure you of your sanity and be there for you when you feel as if you're making the worst choice in the world, even though— despite your self-hating feelings that you're intolerant and getting everything wrong—you are probably taking one of the more helpful decisions of your life.

13
What can you tell me to make me less scared of leaving?

Let us imagine, for the sake of the argument, that you want to leave; it's just that you're scared of doing so. What might you need to hear to lessen the fear? A list might look like this:

1. You are, to a far greater extent than you perhaps realise, already alone. To be formally alone would merely mean concretizing something that has been your reality for a long time anyway and, paradoxically, would be the first step toward helping you to bring the isolation and agonizing frustration to a deserved close.

2. The emotional loneliness you currently feel cannot end until you bring yourself to endure a period of practical loneliness, which is, as you know (but are terrified of knowing), the lesser of the two evils. The awkwardness of dinner by yourself is nothing compared to the challenge of feeling repeatedly misunderstood by a central person in your life. Someone who stubbornly doesn't get it is a greater rebuke to who you are than an empty chair.

3.   You are spending a lot of energy defending yourself against legitimate hope by leaning unfairly on some undoubted general truths: that all lovers are flawed and that all honeymoon periods end. To tease out the limits of this reassuring but ultimately self-deluding exaggeration, change "lovers" to "movies" or "holiday destinations." It is as factually correct to insist that there are no perfect lovers as to point out that there are no perfect movies or resorts. But this is no argument for refusing ever to change TV channels or for denying that there might be an appreciable difference between a vacation in Milton Keynes and one in Lake Como. There is such a thing as "better" and "worse" for you; this truth is no less correct for being difficult to contemplate.

4.   It is worse to be ostensibly together while privately disconnected than to be properly, publicly, firmly by yourself, just as it is better to be allowed to cry than to be forced to smile while burning inside.

5.   What is really holding us back is that we don't trust ourselves very much; we feel undeserving and ashamed of ourselves (this has, as we have started to see, a lot to do with childhood). Our inability to leave is often a symptom of self-hatred. If we were firmly on our own side, it would be more evident that we might deserve and could lay claim to something more sustaining.

6.   Complete the following sentence: "If all the practical hurdles could be taken care of as if by magic (the agony of telling them, the difficulty of finding a new place, the embarrassment of breaking the news to mutual friends, etc.), what I would really like to happen next is ... " Ignoring your reply means sacrificing yet more of your life on the altar of a tricky chat with certain acquaintances who don't care anyway, or of a boring afternoon or two with a real estate agent. Your most precious commodity is time. On deathbeds, no medals are handed out for endurance and a limitless capacity to consume bowls of misery.

7.   The suffering caused by being alone is far easier to endure and assuage than the suffering of a bad relationship. Compared with the appalling impact of squabbles, misunderstandings, bitterness, and coldness, being on your own is not worth any serious concern. The only thing that truly deserves our terror is the prospect of life without a connection to someone we can admire and adore.

8.   You are implicitly assuming that being alone in the future will be an exact replica of how being alone felt before this relationship. Yet your experience in this couple will forever alter how you interpret the discomforts of the single state. The time before you were in this relationship will not be the same as the period that will follow once

you are out of it. Without noticing, silently, you have been acquiring an advanced diploma in compassion, gratitude, and contented aloneness.

9.   Conquering the fear of being alone will be the ultimate guarantee of satisfying love henceforth. People who feel they have no choice make bad choices.

10.   The relationship that is right for you isn't the one without problems, where you won't occasionally be desperate, lose your temper, and behave atrociously. It's one where you will never doubt whether you should really be there. You will be unhappy sometimes, but you'll know in your marrow that you don't secretly long to get out. Fortunately, you will never need to read a book like this again.

14
Does it have to be a tragedy?

News of the end of relationships tends to be greeted with deep solemnity in our societies; we often think of a breakup in terms of a minor tragedy. People will offer condolences as they might after a funeral.

This reflects an underlying philosophy of love. We are taught that the natural and successful outcome of any love story should be to seek to remain with a person until their or our death. By implication, any breakup must be interpreted as a failure on one or both sides.

But there is another scenario in which we understand that we are separating not because our relationship has gone badly, but because it has gone well. It is ending because it has succeeded. Rather than breaking up with feelings of hurt, bitterness, regret, and guilt, we're parting with a sense of mutual gratitude and joint accomplishment.

This counterintuitive but real possibility has an unexpected source. It comes from having kept a crucial question in mind throughout our time together: What is this relationship for? The enquiry may feel negative; we imagine it being asked in a disillusioned tone. But it can, and should, be asked positively and eagerly, with the aim of finding a good answer that goes to the heart of love.

Normally, we imagine love as a kind of ownership. Full of admiration, two people agree to buy one another as they might a static, beguiling object. But there is another, more dynamic and less hidebound way to interpret love: as a particular kind of education. In this view, a relationship comprises a mutual attempt to learn from and teach something to another person. We are drawn to our partners because we want to be educated by them and vice versa; we love them because we see in them things that we long for but that are missing in us; we aspire to grow under the tutelage of love.

For example, a partner might, at the outset, have been confident but also gentle—a combination that, until we met them, had seemed impossible. Or they knew how to laugh at themselves, while we were too withdrawn and solemn to do so. Or they had a practical competence that we found delightful and moving precisely because it was lacking in us. We could accurately say in such cases that the purpose of the relationship was to teach us confidence, or gentleness, or how to laugh at our own idiocy, or how to become more dexterous—or a thousand other qualities, depending on who we both are. The point is that there will have been some specific and important thing we needed to do together that defined what the relationship was for.

By being with the partner, by intertwining our lives, by listening to them, even by being criticized or nagged by them, we will be able gradually to internalize what they have to teach us. But there may come a point where we have absorbed as much from them as we can. Thanks to our partner, we are more mature beings than we were when we got together. We're more balanced and wiser; they've helped us to become more like the people we always wished to be.

Precisely because our relationship has had a great, intimate, loving purpose, it can be completed. It can be finished in the sense in which a novel can be finished— not because the writer got sick of the trials of writing, but because they have, through plenty of difficulties, brought the project to a good resolution. Or—more poignantly, perhaps—a relationship can be finished in the way that childhood can be finished. Thanks to the immense devotion of their parents, a child arrives at a point at which, in order to progress further, they need to leave home. They're not being kicked out in anger or running away in despair; they're leaving because the work of childhood has been done. It is not a rejection of love; it is love's good consequence. Finishing is not a sign of failure but of success.

The difference in these cases is that we've clearly understood what our efforts were for. There was a goal in mind: the writing shouldn't go on forever; the child should leave home. But because we have not asked what our relationship is for, we can't normally get to this sense of having reached a proper ending. Or else we refuse to ask because the only motive for the relationship is to ensure that we are not alone—which, when we reflect on it, is never a good enough reason to monopolize someone else's life.

In an ideal relationship, the sense of completion would be mutual. The painful reality, however, is that we may sometimes want to leave while our partner wants us to stay. But the idea of love as education can still apply: Our unbearable conflicts mean that we've stopped being able to teach one another anything. We may know important qualities they should learn, but we're not the right teacher: We lack the patience, skill, charm, or self-confidence to transmit insights in a way that will work for them. We have done all we can. Our task is complete not because our partner has nothing left to learn, but because we aren't the right person to guide them.

We can avoid feeling devastated by a breakup by knowing that there are many other ways in which we still need to develop. We may have learnt much, but we're still far from complete. It's just that the lessons we now have to take on board will come from someone else—or from the educative experience of being on our own for a while.

15
But I don't find them awful!

One of the reasons we may be confused as to whether to stay or leave is that we don't find our partner especially awful. Remarkably, we don't hate them. Strangely, we don't mind spending time with them. Oddly, we still admire them in a host of ways.

The confusion caused by this duality—by an ongoing respect and tenderness together with a hunch that we should still be off soon—throws up one of the odder, though very prevalent, ideas that circulate in our minds: that the only legitimate moment to leave a person is when we can't bear them any longer; that the primary justification for departure is hatred and a sick feeling in the pit of our stomach; that the reason to quit is loathing.

This idea is unhelpful and cruel for both parties. When we are being left, that story fits into the darkest narrative we may have about ourselves and our value. Of course we are a target of hatred; of course someone has found us despicable. All the sweet words that might have accompanied a breakup must mean nothing. There can only be one reason for the split: The leaver is disgusted with us, has seen something appalling in our soul, considers us vermin, and can't bear our presence. But the story is no less grim for the leaver. It makes what they are doing appear especially cold-hearted. Only a very angry or indifferent person would put a partner through such an event. It raises the stakes of a breakup hugely on both sides.

But, as we have seen, there are a host of far less awful reasons why kind and good people break up: because we need freedom to develop our characters; because we have learnt enough; because we sense that we are stifling someone we love, or are not aligned on some central priorities. It is entirely possible both to quit and to love.

Someone can be wrong now but have been right in all sorts of ways for a very long time. That we still have feelings for our partner is not a sign that we must stay with them; nor is the fact that we are leaving evidence that we must hate them. Tenderness is no unwarranted feeling in a departing partner. If forced, we could happily stay with them for the rest of our lives. But we are not forced, and we are not obliged. Our ultimate responsibility is to our growth and flourishing. We should not be puzzled that we find our partner lovely. We can admire our younger selves for having chosen so wisely, but simultaneously honor who we are today and who we need to be tomorrow.

16
Do I have permission
to do this?

As we contemplate whether to stay or leave, it can help to be alert to an important distinction lurking just beneath the surface of our choice: between what we want to do and what we feel we have permission to do.

It might sound odd to speak of needing permission in this context. We know that, technically, we don't have to ask anyone to act; it's not as if we need to ask God, or our parents, or the authorities. Nevertheless, we may feel—at some odd, semi-unconscious level—as though we couldn't just make a move simply because we alone wanted to. Our own considerations can weigh oddly little in our internal deliberations.

As ever, a look back at the past may prove helpful in explaining our downgrading of ourselves. Many of us grow up with a sense that what we want doesn't rate highly in our priorities. Our early situation may have lent us an impression of danger around pressing our needs forward too vigorously. We may have grown up being used to complying with authority and sacrificing our aspirations in the name of receiving approval or not angering important others. We may be both in touch with what we want and internally bound to ignore our longings in favor of someone else's dictates. Our problem is not that we are confused, but that we haven't evolved the right kind of ruthlessness to look after ourselves.

To liberate ourselves, we might ask ourselves a simple question. We should answer it quickly, without taking much time to think, so as to access our deepest wish:

If you were magically allowed to do whatever you wanted in this situation, what would you do now?

We might try another question, to force ourselves to reckon with the voices of authority that can lurk in the adult mind far longer than they should:

If we could guarantee you that this was alright to do, that it wasn't "bad," that you were allowed to do what you wanted, what would you do?

And finally, for good measure:

What is your secret wish that we, The School of Life, would advise you to do here?

If the answer in all cases is "leave," then the problem is being falsely located. We don't have a stay-or-leave problem; we have a permission problem. We aren't emotionally ambivalent; we're lacking a sense of autonomy and agency. We know what we want, we just don't dare to act on it.

It can be helpful to keep this distinction in mind. We won't then pretend to ourselves or our friends or therapists that we're trying to work out what we're seeking from our relationship; we'll understand that we're in search of "permission" to secure what we already know, in a very shy but very certain bit of our mind, what we are after.

We should have sympathy for ourselves for just how hard it may once have been for us to feel legitimate around our desires. For so long, we might not have felt that we could be respectable, safe, loveable, or good unless we stuck very closely to what other people sought from us: parents, teachers, bosses, and society more broadly. But we are living under a punishing and now unnecessary internal regime. We know what we aspire to; now we have to take a basic step of adult life, to limit our search for permission to the only person we have really needed to consult on this all along: ourselves.

17
Are my expectations too high?

When we contemplate leaving a relationship, it is usually because—in the privacy of our hearts—we harbor expectations of being able to meet another, and in key ways, better kind of person. We are restless inside because we can no longer overlook the shortfalls in the present partner: a problem around emotional intelligence or sexual compatibility, beauty or vigor, wit or kindness. But no sooner have our doubts arisen than we may start to wonder whether we have any right to harbor them. Anyone with a modicum of self-awareness, and therefore insight into their own imperfect and in key ways unattractive selves, is liable to ask: Who are we to complain? Isn't it folly to hope for something better? Should we not merely accept and be grateful for what we have found? How much are we allowed to hope for? Aren't we craving "too much"?

We can start with the good news. The sort of character we are dreaming about does exist somewhere on the earth, probably in multiple incarnations. We're not foolish to picture them. We've probably met approximations of them in many different contexts over the years: on the arm of a friend, in the pages of a magazine, lost in a book opposite us in a café. Let's assume we are not asking for anything plainly crazed (the mind of Einstein in the body of a Hollywood star with the kindness of a saint and the resources of a titan). We are not naïve; we know roughly what we're worth and what we could conceivably attract. We just think—with reason—that we could have a shot at improving on the current candidate. There are seven billion inhabitants on the planet; one or two of them must be able to answer our more ambitious hopes.

Yet none of this is any sort of guarantee. There is enough ill luck, poor timing, and unfortunate happenstance in romantic life to ensure that we may quit our relationship and end up never finding someone who can honor our dreams. Perfectly compatible prospective partners constantly walk past each other and die unfulfilled and alone on opposite sides of the same street. Knowing that there are people out there who could match our criteria says nothing about our chances of finding them in the time that remains.

Therefore, we can never tell anyone who is thinking of leaving their partner that their expectations for a better alternative can be met practically. At best we can eke out a philosophically hedged "perhaps."

But when we wonder whether our expectations are "too high," we might pause and ask something slightly different: Too high for what? If by "too high" we mean too high to be certain that we'll be able to begin a satisfying relationship with a prized candidate, then yes, our expectations may be too high. "Perhaps" is as good as we can get. However, if we're wondering whether our expectations are "too high" to leave our relationship for an uncertain but more honest future, if we're wondering whether it is wrong to define an idea of the kind of person we want and then stick by it whether we actually find them or not, then the answer might be a resounding "no."

In other areas of life, we can accept, and often respect, people who stick by ideas they believe in, even when success doesn't necessarily or immediately follow. There are people who will create a certain kind of art over many decades and pay little attention to whether or not it meets with worldly acclaim. Or who will run a business that doesn't alter its products simply to achieve greater profitability. Or who will stick up for particular ideas in politics, even if this prevents them from reaching high office. They would, of course, always prefer to have the applause, money, and power—but it might be even more important to them to know that they are abiding by the art they believe in, the products they love, and the ideas they identify with.

We would naturally prefer to have what we believe in and the right result from the world, but if it comes down to a choice between dumbed-down art and acclaim, or shoddy products and high profits, or expedient politics and a job in government, or—to shift to the romantic realm—someone to share a bed with but few of the psychological or physical criteria we are truly looking for, then we may prefer to pay the price of loyalty to our original ambitions.

In the context of relationships, there might be two reasons to live like this: the first practical, the second more psychological or existential. At a practical level, there is an advantage in freeing ourselves from a frustrating relationship even in the absence of any immediate prospect of a successful replacement. Being alone gives us a more effective basis for finding love than being shackled to a partner we are surreptitiously looking to edge out. We are free to tell the world what we are seeking; we don't have to lie or hide in the shadows; we won't have to mar the start of a relationship with a messy exit from a previous one.

But beyond this, it may still be wise to abide by our real expectations, whether or not there is a candidate around who can meet them. Our soul is liable to be slowly destroyed by leading a life that privileges mere companionship over companionship in the things we hold dear. We may not be able to escape the consequences to our self-esteem and to our sense of dignity if we know that our fear of being alone has trumped our ability to discriminate in favor of the kind of person who doesn't secretly irritate or bore us. We may no longer like ourselves very much when we daily have to contemplate how far we've drifted from our genuine expectations in order to assuage an ultimately unnecessary terror of our own company.

Japanese history is filled with examples of what commentators have termed "noble failure": people with strong notions of what they respected in a given field (art, politics, business, culture) who remained loyal to their beliefs despite meeting with little or no worldly success, and who sometimes had to pay a great price for their positions. A poet might end their life in obscurity in a hut outside the city; a potter might find their plain but handsome earthenware ignored in favor of more lacquered and showy examples; a politician might see their plans for a better society bar them from advancement at court.

And yet these people could, in the Japanese mind, be viewed as something other than mere "losers." They might, from one perspective, have lost—their art wasn't recognized, their businesses failed, their projects weren't enacted—but they are deemed worthy of respect nevertheless because they had something superior to immediate fame, riches, and applause: clear ideas of what they wanted. Enacted on a far more modest scale over less consequential things, we too may—in romantic life—lean on the concept of noble failure to frame what might occur to us after our exit from a relationship. Our nobility will stem from not allowing our fear of loneliness to govern our conduct and from ensuring that whom we spend time with matches an ambitious concept of human nature—even if this means we are predominantly alone for the long term. We will ultimately prove more loyal to love on our own than we ever could be in the wrong company—just as a lover of music might prefer silence to the wrong kind of background noise.

After exiting a relationship, we may not succeed in any standard way. Our life may look a bit odd. We will have left an apparently sound enough union in order to start a rather arduous existence by ourselves. But we will be something more interesting than merely sad: we will be failing nobly in the pursuit of love; we will have the satisfaction of knowing that we preferred to be alone and true to our hopes than in company yet disloyal to ourselves.

18
How can I tell them?

Let us imagine that we know what we want—to leave a relationship—but that we are suffering from a problem that inhibits us from acting on our wishes: we can't bear to cause another person pain, especially another person toward whom we feel a deep bond, who has been kind to us, who has given us their trust and their future, who has expectations of us, and with whom we might have been planning a trip to another continent in a few months. Perhaps we have come near to telling them on a dozen occasions, but always pulled back at the last moment. We tell ourselves that we'll get around to it "after the holidays," "once their birthday party is over," "next year," "in the morning," and yet the deadlines roll by and we are still here.

Our discomfort has to do with the thought of unleashing an appalling upset: they will dissolve into tears; there will be wailing, uncontrollable cries, and mountains of wet tissues—all because of a truth that currently lurks in the recesses of our cranium. We will be responsible for dragging a formerly competent and independent person into chaos; it's more than we can bear. It sounds peculiar, but it might be better for us to spend the next few decades unfulfilled than to experience even five minutes of unbounded upset. In another part of our minds, there may also be terror. More than we realize day to day, we're scared of our partner. By telling them it's over, we risk a discharge of titanic anger. They may scream at us, accuse us of leading them on, of being a charlatan and a disgrace. There might be violence and danger.

There is a certain symmetry to our fears. We may tell them and, by so doing, kill them. Or we may tell them and they will turn around and kill us—kill or be killed. No wonder we put off delivering the news. The reasonable, adult part of our minds knows that these fears of killing and dying can't be true, but this may weigh very little in how we unconsciously feel. Wielding sensible arguments can, at points, be as effective as telling a person with vertigo that the balcony won't collapse, or a person with depression that there are perfectly good grounds to be cheerful. A lot of the mind is not amenable to surface logic. In an ancestral part of ourselves, we simply operate with a sense that going against the wishes of a significant person will mean either endangering their lives or our own.

Childhood can help to explain the origins of such terrors. Perhaps we are the offspring of a fragile parent whom we loved profoundly and whom it would have broken our hearts to disappoint. They might have been struggling with their mental or physical health; they might have been maltreated by another adult. Maybe they were relying on us to hold them back from despair or to justify their whole lives. We may have derived an early impression that we had to conform to their idea of us if we weren't to cause them grave damage; that our wishes and needs could easily have driven them to the edge; that by being more ourselves we might have broken their spirit. We simply loved them too much, and at the same time felt them to be too weak to ask them to take on our reality. We can be three years old and, without knowing any of this consciously, have taken such messages on board. As a result, we might then have learnt to play very quietly, to rein in our boisterousness or mischievousness, our aggression or our intelligence, to be extremely cheerful and helpful around the house, to be "no trouble at all" toward a beloved adult who already seemed to have too much on their plate.

Alternatively, we might have spent our most impressionable years around a person who responded to any frustration caused by another person with extreme anger. It can be hard to appreciate just how terrifying an enraged adult can seem to a sensitive two-year-old. Another adult might know that this red-faced figure isn't going to murder anyone—they're just letting rip for a while and will pick up the pieces of a smashed vase soon enough—but that's not how it can seem through a child's eyes. How are they to know that a person many times their size won't go one step further and, at the end of their ranting, pick up a hammer and smash their skull in? How can they be certain that the momentarily out-of-control parent who just broke down the door wouldn't throw them out of the window too? Child murder may be alien to the furious adult, but that's not how it can strike a sensitive offspring. A person doesn't have to actually murder anyone to come across as someone who might to an unformed mind. No wonder we might be scared of sharing some awkward news.

Our minds are freighted with fears that stem from things that happened under precise circumstances long ago, but that continue to have a potent, subterranean, scarcely recognized and immense force in our lives today. By taking stock of the past, the task is to acknowledge that these fears are real, but only in a limited place: our own minds. They don't belong to adult reality. The catastrophe we fear will happen has already happened: we have already experienced someone who seemed to risk killing themselves if the news grew too bad, and someone who looked as if they might kill whomever displeased them. But these issues are firmly located in another era. We need to take on board an always unlikely sounding thought: We are now adults, which means there is a robustness to ourselves and to our dealings with others. Another adult is highly unlikely to collapse on us, and if they do, there are plenty of measures we can take. We will know how to help them cope with their grief, directly and indirectly. It may seem as if it will never end, but that is a

child's reasoning, not an adult's. In reality, it will be very
bad for a few hours or days or weeks, but they will get
over it eventually. They will recover their good humor;
they will wake up one morning and see the world hasn't
ended and that they know how to go on. Similarly, they
won't actually try to pick up the nearest ax and chop us
into small pieces. They may be furious, they may shout,
there may be some ugly words, but we are now tall and
independent. We can get away, in extremis we have the
number of the police and a lawyer, we can let the fury vent
and, like a well-built bridge in a hurricane, be confident
that we can withstand whatever tempests come our way.

To further lend us courage, we should remember a
distinction between being kind and seeming kind. It can
look as if the kind thing to do is never to anger or distress
someone—and, therefore, never to give a person we have
loved unwelcome news. But that is to overlook the more
insidious ways in which we can ruin someone's life. To stay
with a person because we wish to avoid unpleasantness
is no favor to them if we go on to be bitter, mean, snide,
unfaithful, and depressed around them for the next few
decades. We're not helping someone by sparing them
a bad breakup scene if we then deliver a lifelong foot-
dragging scene.

A surprising amount of the misery of the world
comes from people being overly keen to appear kind,
or rather being too cowardly to cause others short-term

pain. The truly courageous way to leave is to allow ourselves to be hated for a while by someone who still loves us. We shouldn't imagine that they will never find anyone else like us; they may believe it now and might even sweetly tell us so. But they won't believe it when they finally understand who we are. Real kindness means getting out—even though the vacation has been booked, the apartment paid for, and the wedding arranged. There's nothing wrong with and nothing dangerous about deciding someone isn't for us. There is something very wrong with ruining large chunks of someone else's life while we squeamishly or fearfully hesitate to get out of the way.

19
How come they seem so lovely right now?

Over the years, it's been difficult with our partner. There has been such a long history of harsh words, accusations, insults, shouting, slammed doors, resentments, and aggressive silences.

Let's imagine that it all culminated in a decision to leave. It took us four years to reach this conclusion, or perhaps even longer. There were hours of conversations with friends, therapists, and a lawyer or two. We certainly haven't jumped into this. We made the awkward announcement a few months ago and faced a long period of the partner's hurt and anger. There were some truly horrible scenes. But things have calmed down; the end has turned into a quiet, melancholy, and well-accepted fact on both sides. We're moving out imminently; things are ready with the new apartment; it's the last weekend and we're having a farewell drink before supper.

This is when we start to realize something at once puzzling and a little embarrassing. We acknowledge that we have started to find our about-to-be ex-partner—from whom we have struggled with every sinew to separate at enormous cost and inconvenience—distinctly charming. They're wearing a pair of shoes we like them in; there's a fascinating thing they do with their eyes when they hold their head on one side and shoot a glance at us. We sense their inherent kindness in the way they discuss a mutual acquaintance; their dignity and intelligence is present in their manner of arranging objects around the living room. They say something wry and sharp about an idea they've read in the paper; their mind is very fine. They're lovely. We want to touch their hair, stay longer, unpack the bags, maybe talk to them once more about ... We feel we're having a change of heart at the last moment. We appear to be on the cusp of realizing that we've made a terrible mistake. It's bizarre and contrary to everything we could have predicted, but we're experiencing a powerful attraction to the person we've done everything to try to leave.

What is going on? Is it a genuine reawakening of love and evidence that, if we were to cancel our plans and move back together again, we would now be much happier? Or is this a fervid delusion arising from a temporary mental imbalance with no impact on reality?

We might decode our feelings as follows: We are developing a last-minute crush on the person we're leaving. A classic literary description of a crush can be found in the Russian writer Ivan Turgenev's novel *The Torrents of Spring*, published in 1872. It tells the story of a man who goes into a bar to get a glass of mineral water on the way to the station on a warm spring day. The woman who serves him has delightful hair and a lovely smile and she opens the bottle with unusual grace. He instantly feels he's in love with her and envisages a blissful future for them together. He abandons his journey and books into a nearby hotel so he can be with her all the time. After two days, he decides he must marry her. But after three days, he's realized it was all a terrible mistake—and he runs away and never sees her again.

Although crushes are almost universally associated with the very start of love, in reality they can unfold just as intensely at love's near-end point. In honor of Turgenev's book, we might call our experience with our departing lover a "fall crush."

The essential feature of crushes in both their spring and fall varieties is that, while under their sway, we are not attempting to engage too deeply with the reality of the other person. We are standing outside, peering in respectfully. We are not trying to run a household, get this person to agree with our opinions on politics or family, sex or work, or asking them to love us in a specific way. We're not bringing any of our demands to bear on them. We're merely looking. And from this unpressured vantage point, we register the presence of a properly fascinating and sincerely delightful person. This is a fair judgment on another human, if not necessarily on our chances of being able to maintain a happy relationship with them. Unfortunately, there are far more lovely people in the world than there are ones we might be able to live contentedly alongside.

Although they can seem like ambitious endeavors, crushes are secretly fueled by the lowest of expectations. When we are thinking obsessively of a new person, our demands are running in the background at almost zero. We would be overjoyed if they simply answered our phone call and agreed to see us again. We would feel blessed beyond measure if they held our hand for a minute. We are at an apogee of modesty. But the more the relationship succeeds, the more the criteria on which we judge its success expand. Two months in, we might consider it infuriating or tragic that the partner doesn't want a certain kind of sex with us, misunderstands our family, puts forward a contrary opinion on a friend, or has a clashing taste in interior decoration. We can end up having to finish a relationship not because the partner is awful per se, but because they are disappointing in relation to the elevated expectations for mutuality that we have brought to bear on them over time.

However, it would be unfair to these expectations to dismiss them automatically as pathological or overly demanding. From an objective point of view, they might be entirely legitimate. It is no sign of madness to want to be understood deeply. It does not have to be a delusion to seek out connection and good communication. Our partner might be accomplished in many ways and still not be the person we should be with. During our late crush, we are rediscovering what's nice about someone, not—as we might get muddled into thinking—rediscovering why it might be good to be with them.

If we have decided to leave a partner but suddenly find we desire them once more in the last moments, we should beware of thinking ourselves back in love. We are merely enjoying an artificial rush for someone because we are, finally, on the outside looking in. This is a sign that we have, in a deep part of our souls, finally given up hope of ever trying to live with, or be happy alongside, them.

20
Why do I feel so nostalgic?

After considerable agony, we left the relationship. We're on our own now—and, when we can bear to be honest, it's harder than we expected. We aren't going on many dates; the central heating broke down last week; the shopping is proving a hurdle.

In idle moments, we find ourselves daydreaming, returning fondly to certain occasions in the concluded relationship. There was that wintry weekend by the sea: they looked adorable walking on the beach in their thick scarf. We fed the seagulls and drank cheap white wine from paper cups on the seafront and felt connected and happy. Then there was that moment on vacation in Paris when we discovered the little Vietnamese restaurant hidden away in a side street and became friends with the owner and her husband. Or we recall how, at a large party, we both realized we didn't particularly like the other guests—it was a special, conspiratorial moment: The two of us, shoulder to shoulder, talking over what was wrong with everyone else. We're newly conscious of the charm of so many things that seemed ordinary at the time: coming out of the grocery store and putting everything away in the refrigerator and the cupboards; making soup and grilled cheese and watching television on the couch. With these thoughts in our minds, we feel weepy and tender—perhaps even tempted to call the ex again. They would, we suspect, allow us back, or at least give us a hearing.

What can we make of our feelings? It might be that we have realized a genuine mistake. But it's even more likely that we are in the grip of a characteristic mental habit of the newly single, facing the vertigo of independence: nostalgia.

In the mid-19th century, Britain underwent industrial and scientific revolutions that transformed old, settled ways of life, ripping apart communities, throwing people together in large and anonymous cities, and dislocating the loyalties and certainties once offered by religion. In a search for ways to soften the confusion, artists and thinkers began to imagine what a better world might look like. In certain circles, the search turned toward the past and, more specifically, to the perceived wisdom, coherence, and contentment of the Middle Ages. While railway lines were being laid down across the land, and telegraph cables under the seas, members of the artistic class celebrated the simple, innocent communities that, they proposed, had existed in the 12th and 13th centuries. Artworks depicted handsome, uneducated but happy laborers, cheerful villagers celebrating harvests, and kindly lords and ladies ministering to the deserving poor. In their version, there seemed to be no violence, alienation, fear, or cruelty. No one minded not having much heating or subsisting on a meager diet of oats and the odd chunk of lard. It was alleged that life was much easier back then, in the thatched cottages and pious stone churches.

At the heart of this nostalgic attitude was a disregard for why things ever changed—and might have needed to do so. For the nostalgic, the past never required alteration or development; history moved on for no sane reason. The complexities of the present moment are, in this sense, deemed accidental. They are not the tricky by-products of a legitimate search for growth and progress away from what must have been, at some level, despite the odd delightful occasion (perhaps at harvest time or on a midsummer morning), an intolerable previous arrangement. The nostalgic can't accept that the present—whatever its faults—came about because of inescapable difficulties with the past. They insist that we were once perfectly happy, then mysteriously changed everything for the worse because we forgot we had been so.

Relationships can find us reasoning no less selectively. Here, too, it can feel as if we must once have been content and then grew ungrateful through error and inattention. Yet in locating profound satisfaction in the past, we are crediting our earlier selves with too little acumen. The truth about what a relationship is like is best ascertained not when we are feeling low six months or a few years after its conclusion, but from what we must have known when we were in its midst, when we were most familiar with all the facts upon which we made our slow and deliberate decisions.

The specific grounds for our dissatisfactions tend to evaporate. We edit out the rows, the botched trips, the sexual frustrations, the stubborn standoffs. The mind is squeamish. It doesn't like to entertain bad news unless there is a present danger to attend to. But knowing our amnesiac tendencies, we can be certain that profound unpleasantness must have existed, for there would otherwise have been no explanation for our decision to rip our situation apart. We would not have needed to act if things had been as gratifying as we are now nostalgically assuming they were. The portrait we are painting of the relationship is emerging not from knowledge but from loneliness and apprehension.

Furthermore, our sense of ourselves as people who could be satisfied with what was on offer is as untrue to our own nature as is the fantasy of a modern urban dweller dreaming they might find enduring happiness in a medieval wooden hut. The solution to the problem of satisfying our complicated needs is not to hallucinate that they don't exist. It is to square up to them and use all our ingenuity to devise workable solutions for them.

We should trust not what we feel now, in our weepy, disconsolate state, but what we must have known then. A simple guideline emerges: We must trust the decisions we took when we had the maximal information to hand upon which we made them—not when we have emotional incentives to change our minds. There were persuasive reasons, even if, in our sadness, we now can't remember a single one. Returning to the past would not make us content; it would merely remind us why change was so necessary. We should have the courage of our true and complex natures, and be ready to pay the full price for them.

21

Is it okay to compromise?

We reserve some of our deepest scorn for couples who stay together out of compromise: those who are making a show of unanimity, but who we know are not fully happy. Maybe they're together because of the children; maybe they're sticking around because they're scared of being lonely; maybe they're just worried that anyone else they found wouldn't be much better.

These seem like disgraceful motives to be with anyone—disgraceful on account of a background belief that circulates powerfully through the collective modern psyche: that there are pain-free, profoundly fulfilling options available for all of us, and the only things that could stand in the way of discovering them would be laziness and cowardice, flaws of character that deserve no particular sympathy or forgiveness. Our Romantic expectations have made us impatient around, and censorious about, those who can't attain them.

But imagine if we were to tweak the premise of the argument a little and, for a moment, probe at the notion that there really might be a pain-free and fulfilling option available for all of us at all times. What if our choices were, in fact, rather more limited than Romanticism proposes? Maybe there aren't as many admirable, unattached people in our vicinity as there might be. Maybe we lack the charm, the personality, the career, the confidence, or the looks ever to attract the ones that do exist. Maybe time is running out. Or maybe our children would take it badly if we dynamited the family for the sake of better sex and greater cheer elsewhere.

At the same time, maybe the current situation—although a compromise—has some virtues.

A partner may be only half right, quite often maddening and properly disappointing in certain areas, but—crucially—a vital companion in others. Having children to bring up together may be worth it even with a co-parent about whom one has a long, only semi-private, list of reservations. A few cuddles, occasional moments of coziness, and shared history may retain a small but decisive edge over conclusive abandonment interspersed with humiliating dates.

The capacity to compromise is not always the weakness it is sometimes described as being. It can involve a mature, realistic admission that there may simply be no ideal options in certain situations. Conversely, an inability to compromise does not always have to be the courageous and visionary position it is held to be by our impatient and perfectionist ideology: it may just be a slightly rigid, proud, and cruel delusion.

Mocking people who compromise is, of course, emotionally handy. It localizes a problem that it is normal to want to disavow. It pins to a few scapegoat couples what we fear in our relationships: that a degree of sadness may just be an intrinsic and unavoidable part of them.

Wiser societies would be careful never to stigmatize the act of compromise. It is painful enough to have to compromise; it is even more painful to have to hate yourself for having done so. We should rehabilitate and occasionally honor the ability to put up with a flawed fellow human being, to nurse our sadness without falling into rage or despair, to reconcile ourselves to our damaged appearance and character, and to accept that there may be no better way for us to live but partly in pain and longing, given who we are and what the world can provide. Couples who compromise may not, in reality, be the sworn enemies of love; they may be at the vanguard of understanding what staying the course in a relationship can demand.

22
How do I find closure?

At the root of many malfunctioning relationships and unhappy breakups lie two stories that run alongside one another but never manage to align or converge, about who has done what to whom and why. In the mind of one of the participants, the reason why, after so many fights and frustrated evenings, matters eventually had to come to an end might be summarized like this:

> *My partner was cold: I tried so hard to ask them for greater emotional connection, but they always became defensive and eventually I had to give up to preserve my sanity.*

But in the mind of the other partner (who might have spent five years in the very same bed as them), the story of exactly the same relationship might sound very different:

> *My partner was demanding and paranoid, always suspecting that I didn't love them. But I did! Just in a different way. They kept getting furious and frustrated with me, and eventually that became impossible.*

It is gratifying to have to hand a story of a breakup that feels familiar, that positions us in a benevolent light and that casts doubt on the integrity of the departed lover. But unless a story can also in some way be corroborated by its cocreator, there is likely to be an enduring problem for both partners psychologically. We will be left feeling strangely dissatisfied, uneasy, questioning and, in our more courageous moments, skeptical as to whether we have really understood what happened and why we failed. We will have left, but, as the expression puts it, we will be lacking "closure."

Closure doesn't involve magically eradicating all differences between two stories, but harmonizing the points of view into a more generous joint narrative that holds room for alternate realities.

The difficulty of life without closure is that one or the other party must be entirely right and the other, by necessity, entirely wrong, as if love were a court of law where the outcome had to be binary, and either someone would be wholly guilty or they would be wholly exonerated. So, in the case of our imagined story, either one partner was unnaturally cold and the other completely reasonable in the way they tried to build intimacy, or else the allegedly cold partner was in fact thoroughly sane and it was their partner who was in every way peculiar in the intensity of their demands. This sterile debate may go on for years within the couple—and then in each person's mind for decades after the breakup.

Part of why we cannot rest easy is that we suspect that any story that feels too gratifying and too flattering to our own interests must only ever be half a story—and half-stories have an unfortunate habit of not allowing us to sleep as well as we should. The choice is between clinging to a sense of being unquestionably "right," or of allowing ourselves to understand the reality of love.

The true story of the relationship, told from an Olympian vantage point by a warm-hearted narrator, will always involve a judicious blend of sympathies. Without knowing any of the specifics, we can be sure that the direction will be toward nuance and ambiguity. Yes, the partner was in certain ways at the colder end of things, but let's call this emotional avoidance rather than coldness, as that term deserves sympathy and is understandable, given their complicated and painful early history. And of course, the way the other person handled that tendency was not especially admirable. Shouting "Show me some affection, you weirdo!" is a paradoxical request at the best of times. Then again, it would be fairer to say that this afflicted character wasn't just mean; they were anxiously attached—a phenomenon that also has a history and carries with it plenty of grounds for compassion.

It takes great courage to surrender a tenacious hold on an overly neat story and to wonder whether what's written down in an ex's "book" might hold one or two truths that we could benefit from assimilating. But when we dare to surrender full control and feel confident enough to cast ourselves in a not entirely heroic light, we will come into possession of something even more important than a neat story: a multifaceted, intelligent, kind, and resolved one.

23
Are there alternatives to staying or leaving?

When it comes to what sort of relationships we are offered, our societies tend to present us with a menu with only one option: the monogamous, cohabiting Romantic relationship, usually served with a side order of children. To be considered normal, we are meant to develop overwhelming emotional and sexual feelings for one very special person, who will then become a combination of our best friend, sole sexual partner, co-parent, business associate, therapist, travel companion, property co-manager, kindergarten teacher, and soulmate—and with whom we will live exclusively in one house, in one bed, for many decades, in substantial harmony, and with an active tolerance for each other's foibles and ongoing desire for their evolving appearance, till death do us part.

But what is striking, for an arrangement supposed to be normal, is how many people cannot abide by its rules. At least half flunk completely, and a substantial portion muddle along in quiet desperation. At best, only around fifteen percent of the population admit to being totally satisfied—a thought-inducingly low figure for a menu option claiming universal validity.

In our societies, those who can't get on with Romantic monogamous marriage are quickly diagnosed as suffering from a variety of psychological disorders: fear of intimacy, clinginess, sexual addiction, frigidity, boundary issues, self-sabotage, childhood trauma, etc. We powerfully imply that someone might be psychologically ill if they don't want to keep having sex exclusively with the same partner, or seek to spend every other weekend apart, or want to develop a close friendship elsewhere.

But the reason why we may find it so hard to know whether to stay in or leave a relationship isn't that there is one answer that, mysteriously and stupidly, we simply can't locate. It's that no existing answer is actually appealing. This is an insight that our Romantic culture refuses to help us to contemplate with the clarity it deserves. We don't want fully to leave, and we don't want fully to stay. Yet we push this thought away because it sounds impossible and spoilt. How could we possibly stay and not stay at the same time? However, perhaps this mad-sounding wish is actually very sane, because it picks up on a hidden error in our thinking—that we have only two options.

We'd recognize this instantly if someone said: "You have to make a choice: You can either go on a beach vacation and swim for six hours every day, or you can go to a city, but it has to be Geneva. Don't be indecisive! Which will it be?" It would be reasonable to be maddened by the options: Why just these specific packages? The beach could be lovely, but why so much swimming? A city could be marvelous, but why does it have to be Geneva?

The problem deciding lies not in us, but in the choices we're being offered.

The Romantic model is so familiar that we easily forget that it's a very particular and recent amalgam of roles that have in the past, and could again in the future, exist independently. We might liberate ourselves from the harsh dichotomy by looking at a few alternatives to staying or leaving.

i.

Erotic friendship

In 1745, the king of France, Louis XV, invited Jeanne Antoinette Poisson (soon to be ennobled and called by her more recognizable name, Madame de Pompadour) to be his "official" mistress. He installed her in a grand apartment and, for the next few years, spent most afternoons and many nights in her company.

This was not a secretive arrangement; Madame de Pompadour became enormously influential because everyone knew of her deep intimacy with the king. And it was not seen as a threat to his marriage; there was no question of a divorce, and, in fact, the queen and Madame de Pompadour became good friends.

The idea of a publicly respectable mistress was based on a view about marriage: it was accepted that there might be many excellent reasons for two people to be married, but that these wouldn't necessarily include great personal closeness. This is what had happened with Louis. While still in his teens, he married Princess Marie Leczinska of Poland. She was an excellent partner in many ways: they had lots of children together; she was very religious and was popular with the wider public; she was also a helpfully neutral figure between the contending political factions at court. These were not minor considerations, and Louis never regretted marrying her.

The thing that strikes us as strange, but that is potentially so helpful to consider, is that a relationship might be healthy and successful yet involve one or both (to update the story) of the partners sleeping with other people. The crucial foundation is that the couple is very clear about other reasons why they are together. The grounds for their union are so compelling, and the basis of respect and admiration is so strong, that there's no great need to worry about whom else the other person might, quite regularly, be spending the early evening or weekend afternoons with.

ii.

The parenting couple

When it comes to the children, two people might be fully united. They're both there at dinner time; they share the ritual of the evening bath and the bedtime story; they're both around at breakfast; they take family vacations together. But other than that, they live independent lives. They're not checking who is seeing whom or what the other is doing on Tuesday afternoons; they don't feel ownership of each other's existence. They have separated their finances and don't talk much about anything other than the children.

They're not staying together "for the sake of the children" (an always uncomfortable arrangement), because they aren't genuinely together. They have separated—just not entirely because there's still one very important task they're undertaking together and will continue to for many years.

In the past, the two used to squabble or be frosty with one another in front of the children because their role as parents was embedded in a highly unsatisfactory relationship as partners. Now they're more focused and serene. Letting go of expectations for true intimacy and understanding has freed them to be kind and respectful of one another as they prepare supper.

iii.
The companion

While still married, you also have a special friend. It's not sexual: you're not mutually attracted, so you're not tempted to have an affair with them. But you speak to them more or less every day and discuss the details of your life; you see them frequently and help each other in lots of ways. Your companion might sit down with you and go through paying the bills or you might assemble some flat-pack furniture together. It's like friendship, but it moves into areas that we've wrongly come to see as the exclusive realm of what couples are supposed to do together.

This kind of arrangement has been formalized at various times and in different places. In Japan, a man might spend some evenings with a geisha. No sex would be on offer—perhaps only mild flirtation. Rather, the geisha is a specialist in the arts of entertainment and conversation: a witty sympathetic listener who can lighten the mood or capture a delicate thought.

Or in Italy, in the 18th century, a noble woman might have had a cavaliere, or "knight": a male companion who would be charming and kind; they'd have lunch together, go shopping, attend parties; when the lady went traveling to visit friends in the country, the cavaliere would accompany her and ensure the carriage was loaded up with some agreeable snacks for the journey.

In essence, the idea is to separate out companionship from the rest of a relationship. It doesn't mean the couple has no contact, just that differences in temperament don't become unbearable. Your primary partner may be very good in all sorts of ways, but they are so busy, or they hate shopping, or they aren't much of a conversationalist.

Normally, these points of incompatibility could be fatal. But they needn't be with the right companion in one's life.

iv.
The sex club

It's a rainy Wednesday night; in a darkened room, discreetly tucked away in a side street, a logistics manager is being flogged by a trainee architect, and a retired engineer is putting a leash round the neck of a marketing executive. Most of these people are married, but they're here without their partners.

At the club, sex is detached from intimacy. The participants know almost nothing about each other— perhaps not even their names. They don't have long, flirtatious conversations or swap phone numbers. It can sound brutish because we'd ideally like sex to be closely aligned with love. But in reality, some of us develop highly specific erotic desires. It's not a matter of choice: we just discover that we're immensely excited by wearing a rubber costume or by being loudly sworn at. The thought of never doing these things makes us miserable.

Yet for entirely valid and comprehensible reasons, our partner might be unable to participate in these activities. We've tried gentle suggestions; we've explained our interest as best we can. It's not a question of good will: Our partner is left utterly cold by such ideas. Our relationship might be fine in many other important ways, but the distress that can accumulate around this one area may put everything under strain, which is a great pity.

The Romantic model of relationships ineluctably drives us toward a tragic decision: Either we stay in the union, but have to accept that an important part of our soul isn't going to be understood, or we have to abandon everything that's good and important in our relationship for the sake of a few hours of pleasure every week.

The sex club rejects this binary choice. It offers to target a precise erotic longing, but only that. And by so doing, it can liberate us to properly appreciate everything else that's right and intimate in our relationship.

v.

The holiday marriage

Instead of living together all year round, this couple spends most of their time apart—but they get together for two weeks over New Year and longer in the summer, and maybe a couple of other times. It's a long-term commitment. They do it year after year and wouldn't think of breaking the arrangement. When they're together, they go out to dinner, they are warm to each other, and they have long, intimate conversations.

These are people who feel deeply connected to one another, but who have realized that living together most of the time is agony. They were at odds over what color to paint the bathroom walls, what time to get up in the morning, whether to live in the city or the country, whether each was pulling their weight financially, and how to divide up the domestic chores. Sex might not have been very good either. The holiday model frankly admits that living together continuously is unbearable, but it doesn't take this as the end of the relationship. Instead it separates the quotidian frustrations from the underlying question of closeness or love.

* * *

These alternative options might look like second best— an embarrassing climb-down from what we're supposed to really want, which is the unified relationship in which a couple does everything together. But that might not actually be what we, ourselves, long for. The Romantic model was a deliberate, difficult creation. Starting in the late 18th century, particularly in France, a very few people decided that what they most desired was a relationship in which everything was shared and in which their domestic companion was also their lover. They were regarded as freakish and unnatural. But over time they portrayed their ideals so eloquently and beautifully in poems, paintings, sermons, novels, and plays that this way of having a relationship came to seem like a universal obligation.

But it is, in fact, quite odd that we take there to be just one single model of what a proper relationship should be like. We don't impose this type of standard measure on ourselves in other areas of existence. We don't think there is just one kind of ideal job that everyone must have, or one kind of good vacation, or one type of house that everyone should live in. In general, we're much more flexible in recognizing that our own needs might vary quite a lot from the statistical norm and yet not be any less valid or authentic.

When we're struggling with the question "Stay or leave?," we may, behind the scenes, be doing something surprisingly creative. We're trying to imagine how we would really like to live with a person whom we love, but who (like everyone) is radically imperfect in some ways and cannot fathom important parts of us. As with so many creative acts, the ideas we come up with will, at first, sound very strange. Like those who evolved the idea of the Romantic model, we are pioneers. We're trying to define as carefully and as plausibly as we can why some as-yet-unfamiliar way of living might, in practice, be the best arrangement for us.

It would be a genuine liberation if, whenever a new couple came together, it was assumed that they almost certainly would not go along with the Romantic, monogamous template, and that the onus was therefore on them to discuss—up front, in good faith and without insult—the alternative arrangements that would ideally satisfy their natures. Extra marks would be awarded for innovation and out-of-the-box schemes, while protestations of satisfaction at the standard model would raise eyebrows.

Once upon a time, male offspring of the European upper classes had only two career options: to join the army or to join the church. Such narrow-mindedness was eventually dismissed as evident nonsense and eradicated; the average citizen of a developed country now has at least 4,000 job options to choose from. We should strive for a comparable expansion of our menus of love. We are not so much bad at relationships as unable to understand our needs without shame, to stick up politely for what makes us content, and to invent practical arrangements that could stand a chance of honoring our complex emotional reality.

24
Am I making a terrible mistake?

Everything in this book has centered on trying to help us minimize error and subsequent regret. There is an enormous amount we can do to clarify our thinking and reduce our chances of acting blindly and against our deeper interests. But at a certain moment, there is also a need to face up to a reality that, once we have embraced it fully, may also prove remarkably cheering: that whatever we do will, in some ways, be slightly wrong.

Any step we take will end up with certain regrets. We might leave and suffer; we might stay and suffer. We might even invent a new arrangement—and suffer still. Wholly suffering-free choices don't exist. We simply don't have the luxury of never losing out when we make a choice.

The person who understood this bracing truth best was the 19th-century philosopher Søren Kierkegaard, whose thought revolved around the idea of a fundamental incompleteness to all our lives. Any one choice, asserted Kierkegaard, will cut us off from other choices in which certain forms of happiness could have been found; we are condemned to an occasional and true feeling of having missed out on our best opportunities. In a bleakly comedic passage in his *Either/Or*, Kierkegaard tried to shake us from our attachment to the idea of being able to make choices without suffering any penalties:

> Marry, and you will regret it; don't marry, you will also regret it; marry or don't marry, you will regret it either way. Laugh at the world's foolishness, you will regret it; weep over it, you will regret that too; laugh at the world's foolishness or weep over it, you will regret both. Believe a woman, you will regret it; believe her not, you will also regret it ... Hang yourself, you will regret it; do not hang yourself, and you will regret that too; hang yourself or don't hang yourself, you'll regret it either way; whether you hang yourself or do not hang yourself, you will regret both. This, gentlemen, is the essence of all philosophy.

It may sound brutal, but it is in fact very kind (and, like many true and dark things, very funny). We should not torture ourselves with an idea of an idyll we might miss out on. Whatever we do will, in the nicest and kindest possible way, leave us a bit unhappy, feeling that we should have acted in another way and beset with sadness for something we have (genuinely) missed out on. This won't be a sign that we have made the "wrong" choice (there is often no such thing in these matters, and no fully "right" one either)—just that we are, in all our glory and idiocy, enduring the actual conditions of existence. The lesson is to lower our expectations of being able to choose with perfect wisdom, or to inoculate ourselves against all regret. Of course we'll get this one slightly wrong, but it needn't be just a tragedy. In the right mood, it might also be a subject for laughter, consoling friendship, and the best sort of despairing humility in the face of the thorny dilemmas life reliably puts in our way.

Also available from The School of Life:

The School of Life: Relationships

Learning to love

A book to inspire closeness and connection, helping people not only to find love but to make it last.

Few things promise us greater happiness than our relationships. Yet few things make us more miserable and frustrated. What are we doing wrong? For one thing, we forget that we aren't born knowing how to love. Love isn't always intuitive, and it's not always easy.

Love is a skill to be learned, rather than just an emotion that is felt. This book calmly (and charmingly) takes us through all the key issues of relationships—from arguments to sex, forgiveness to communication—making sure that success in love need never again be just a matter of luck.

ISBN: 978-1-915087-13-3

Also available from The School of Life:

The Couple's Workbook

Homework to help love last

Therapeutic exercises to help couples nurture patience, forgiveness, and humor.

Love is a skill, not just an emotion—and in order for us to get good at it, we have to practice, as we would in any other area we want to shine in.

Here is a workbook containing the very best exercises that any couple can undertake to help their relationship function optimally—exercises to foster understanding, patience, forgiveness, humor, and resilience in the face of the many hurdles that invariably arise when you try to live with someone else for the long term.

The goal is always to unblock channels of feeling and improve communication. Not least, doing exercises together is—at points—simply a lot of fun.

ISBN: 978-1-912891-26-9

Also available from The School of Life:

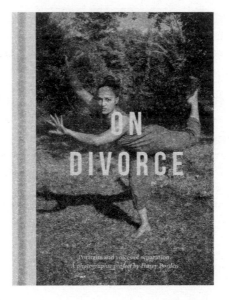

On Divorce

Portraits and voices of separation: A photographic project by Harry Borden

An intimate photographic study on the subject of divorce by Harry Borden and The School of Life.

Everyone wants to talk about weddings; few can bear to consider divorce. But as divorce is the ultimate outcome of around half of all marriages, the topic cries out for fresh consideration and illumination.

This is a visually captivating and psychologically stirring book that restores divorce to its deserved status as a subject of complexity and interest.

Through 48 evocative portraits and poignant interviews by the renowned photographer Harry Borden, readers are introduced to a diverse array of individuals, spanning different ages and backgrounds, whose lives have in some way been impacted by divorce.

This is a book for anyone who has ever been through divorce or might somewhere along the line encounter it—that is, for anyone who has ever dared to love.

ISBN: 978-1-915087-39-3

Also available from The School of Life:

THE SCHOOL OF LIFE

Why You
Will Marry the
Wrong Person

Why You Will Marry the Wrong Person

We are all desperate, of course, to marry the right person. But none of us ever quite does. The fault isn't entirely our own; it has to do with the difficult truth that anyone we're liable to meet is going to be rather wrong, in some fascinating way or another, because this is simply what all humans happen to be—including, sadly, ourselves. Yet—as these darkly encouraging and witty essays propose—we don't need perfection to be happy. So long as we enter our relationships in the right spirit, we have every chance of coping well enough with, and even delighting in, the inevitable and distinctive wrongness that lies in ourselves and our beloveds.

ISBN: 978-0-9955736-2-8

The School of Life publishes a range of books on essential topics in psychological and emotional life, including relationships, parenting, friendship, careers, and fulfillment. The aim is always to help us to understand ourselves better and thereby to grow calmer, less confused, and more purposeful. Discover our full range of titles, including books for children, here:

www.theschooloflife.com/books

The School of Life also offers a comprehensive therapy service, which complements, and draws upon, our published works:

www.theschooloflife.com/therapy

THESCHOOLOFLIFE.COM